How to Get Your Resisting Loved One into Treatment

A Step-by-Step Plan for Mental Health and/or Addiction Crisis

Critical knowledge and skills to get your struggling loved one on a path to recovery

Brian F. Licuanan, PhD

ISBN 979-8-9878309-8-7 (paperback)
ISBN 979-8-9878309-9-4 (ebook)

Published by BL Press and Publications

What mental health experts, clinicians, and family members are saying about *How to Get Your Resisting Loved One into Treatment: A Step-by-Step Plan for Mental Health and/or Addiction Crisis*

"Dr. Licuanan's book is a breath of fresh air among books, articles, and treatments pertaining to addiction, offering practical and specific strategies for how to help a loved one in need. Dr. Licuanan's work is honest about the individual, family, and systems challenges in addiction and mental health treatment, and it offers the hope paired with discipline that families desperately need at this time."

—Dr. Lynette Sparkman-Barnes, Psy.D, Clinical Psychologist, Multicultural Specialist, Associate Director, The University of Kansas Medical Center

"Dr. Licuanan's book is one I wish I had when our son was struggling with addiction and depression. This disease is hard on the entire family unit, and a guide like this can ease the worry and give hope to those who want only the best for their struggling loved one."

—Christine V., parent of child in recovery for ten years

"I have worked in the field of addiction and mental health for 30 years, and Dr. Licuanan's book is valued and needed. I respect his experience and wisdom, as I also had the honor of working with him on a clinical team years ago. He is naturally gifted with sincere compassion. It is not easy working with this milieu. Thank you for caring!"

—Crystal M. Ornelas, BS, CADCII, ICADC

"Dr. Licuanan's book was a very easy read and addresses core issues many people struggle with today. His examples, tools, and tips make it easy to identify how to help your patient/loved one. I wish I had this resource years ago to help me understand addiction/mental illness and all the accompanying dynamics. You are amazing! You clearly love what you do!"

—Tanya Brown, life coach and author of Finding Peace Amid the Chaos: My Escape from Depression and Suicide

"Excellent resource for families and loved ones with individuals struggling with addiction and mental health conditions. A thoughtful approach to offer support with appropriate boundaries and help loved ones engage in appropriate care and treatment."

—*Anna Molnar, M.D., psychiatrist*

"*How to Get Your Resisting Loved One into Treatment* is the missing resource family members have needed when it comes to navigating chronic mental health issues. This will be an invaluable tool for anyone who wants to better understand individuals who require long-term recovery."

—*Meghan Marcum, PsyD, ABPP, Chief*
Psychologist at AMFM Treatment

"This book is a great guide on how to get someone who is struggling with their disease into treatment and onto the road to recovery. It is practical, simple, and relatable."

—*Bernadette H., PMHNP, husband Dave, six years sober*

"Dr. Licuanan's book addresses several issues that families struggling to get their loved one into treatment are experiencing. This is a clear and precise step-by-step guide with professional and clinical approaches that fills a huge gap for families who are living in the deepest depths of mental illness and addiction with their loved ones, presenting the answer to disrupt and end the destructive behaviors that cause so much pain. This guide can support families to heal and restore the relationships and family dynamics impacted by their loved one's unhealthy coping mechanisms and present glimpses of hope for a happy and healthy life. This book is by far the most important tool to aid in your "quest to cure" your loved one and get them into treatment and save your sanity."

—*Tara Zelmer, health and lifestyle coach for Wellness*
and Recovery, Health Solutions Partners Inc.

"Although it can feel discouraging when a loved one refuses to get help for their mental health condition, family members are not without options. This book provides you with critical information on how to help your loved one enter treatment, expectations for their recovery journey, and recommendations for helping them sustain long-term management of their mental health condition(s)."

—Danielle Portney, LMFT

"This book gives a beacon of hope to the families struggling with a loved one suffering from a current state of despair due to chemical dependency/addiction. If you are struggling, stressed, and confused but don't know where to start in the process of getting that loved one into treatment and on to long term stabilization/recovery, then I highly recommend this book."

—Cameron H., sober for ten years

Disclaimer: This book contains recommendations and advisory tips not intended to be universally prescriptive for all families in crisis. Furthermore, the recommendations do not guarantee any specific outcomes. It is also worth noting that there are other possible approaches and strategies to get your loved one the help they may need, and this guide is just one potential path to doing so. The knowledge in this book can be integrated as a supplementary guide in developing your finalized plan. I highly encourage you to consult with your therapist or other healthcare professionals in devising the best strategy for the needs of your loved ones and your family.

For those of us who survived the life-changing, unforgettable year for humanity, a year when I humbly discovered a near-impossible, silver lining during the tragic, global pandemic— without which this book would not have been possible.

For everyone who has lost a loved one to the diseases of mental health and substance use, and for those who refuse to give up the fight.

With thanks to Dad and Mom, for always believing and never giving up on me, and to Jay and Tiff, for your unconditional acceptance and support.

For my wife, Tina, for her unending love, and my two children, Chloe and Christian, the reasons I work so hard to make an impact on the world.

Contents

Introduction

First and foremost, thank you for trusting me to be part of your family's solution in getting your loved one into treatment. If you are reading this book, perhaps the chances are someone dear to you is tirelessly struggling to manage his or her mental health conditions and/ or substance use and most probably refusing help. Maybe your family has pulled out all the stops— limitless compassion, soft love, tough love, validation, strict rules, flexible rules, collaboration, partnering, empathy, agreements—but nothing is working. Perhaps it seems you are out of options to help your loved one get better, yet you aren't ready to give up hope. You may be a clinician or friend wanting to support a client or colleague. Or you may be an educator who wants to integrate this knowledge into your curriculum. No matter how or why you found your way here, I appreciate your willingness to be a critical part of the solution in battling this beatable disease. You are on the right path, increasing your chances for success by seeking help and not giving up.

In my practice, countless numbers of families have come to me for assistance. I've heard story after story from people desperate for ways to get their struggling family members the help they need. One day after a tough family session (we were finally able to get a son into treatment after a bout with marijuana-induced psychosis), I realized I've been reiterating the same message and approaches to families for years. As a result, I decided to write this strategy guide, a resource to reach a wider range of families.

So many families contact me believing they are out of tools and options, feeling as if their hands are tied behind their backs. Common complaints include:

- "We have tried everything, and nothing works."
- "We are scared because our loved one not only struggles with substance abuse disorder, but also bipolar disorder/major depressive disorder/suicidality /schizophrenia, etc."
- "We're not getting specific guidance about getting help for our loved ones. We are given general advice, such as 'Use tough love,' 'You need to set firm boundaries,' 'Stop enabling,' etc. We need *How To* suggestions for implementing these recommendations."
- "Our loved one doesn't think she has a problem, refuses help, and resists any type of assistance."
- "He suffers from anosognosia, so he has no insight into his condition!"
- "We feel stuck in a paradox and wonder whether our loved one is better off at home, unhealthy yet safe—or out on the streets, in jail, or homeless."

The first thing I tell families is *there is always hope*. Without hope, the fight is already lost. Helping your loved one get healthier will require work, perhaps some of the toughest you've ever encountered. It will take an emotional and mental toll. Remember that getting your unwell family member help doesn't mean you will stop loving and caring for them; it merely means you need to change your approach and strategy. As mentioned earlier, there are many different approaches and strategies to getting your loved one help. For instance, I will discuss later in Chapter 6 (Flattening the Risk Curve) my thoughts on whether or not harm reduction is an option. Briefly, harm reduction is a public health strategy which certain techniques are used to reduce the negative effects of concerning behaviors (e.g., drinking daily three cans of beer rather than a bottle of vodka, providing clean syringes to intravenous drug users to prevent spread of diseases, scratch arms with a semi-dull knife rather than a razor blade for a person with self-cutting tendencies) as a way to move towards healthier recovery when complete abstinence is not feasible.

In my clinical work, I have seen disheartening cases—severe mental health acuities and extremely dysfunctional family dynamics—but people in these dire situations can navigate a healthier path when every person in the intimate support system does their part. Time and again, I've witnessed how devastating the diseases of mental illness and substance abuse can be to family infrastructures, tearing away at the fabric of loving relationships and fracturing the closest of familial networks. However, when a family goes through treatment, members are often able to reestablish intimacy, repair long-lasting feuds, melt away years of estrangement, and solidify a unified front that is stronger than ever before. Ironically, the same disease that tore a family apart can be the catalyst that brings them back together, through the treatment process. Families unite when they realize the best way to fight is to let the disease know it's no longer welcome.

As critical as it is to get your loved one help, I can't emphasize enough how paramount it is to also prioritize your own recovery and healing—in other words, Take Care of Yourselves! If you are not healthy yourself, helping a loved one is extremely difficult. As I will explain later, each family member intimately involved in the treatment process needs to accept and diligently work on their shared portion of accountability. This sharing of responsibility increases the overall chances of success not only for the individual but for the family unit as a whole. Some examples of ways you can help yourself are participating in individual therapy, joining a support group, seeking life coaching, creating a healthy fellowship, conducting personal audits (self-check-ins), working with a provider for medication management as needed, spending time with friends, taking big or small get-aways, participating in an extracurricular activity (e.g., church functions, philanthropy positions, volunteer opportunities), etc. Though this book does not directly delve into specific strategies for self-care for family members, many of the recommendations may speak indirectly to caring for yourselves (e.g., setting interpersonal boundaries, improving communication skills, recognizing hope in despair). I strongly urge you to seek professional guidance if you feel the need for additional support.

Most importantly, I hope you walk away from this book with a renewed belief that you can help your suffering family member return to their healthier, better self. It's never too late for your loved one to start a new life chapter. I hope this guide serves as the first step in making those transformations by illustrating the essential knowledge and actions necessary to commence the change process.

Chapter 1
Author's Objectives and Perspective

My objectives

1. Understand the patterns and attributes of the disease.
2. Identify dysfunctional patterns on the individual and family level.
3. Learn how to set healthy boundaries.
4. Improve communication skills.
5. Understand healthy roles in the recovery process.
6. Utilize the procedural steps to get your loved one help.
7. Recognize the attributes of a strong recovery program.

My perspective

This chapter is also meant to help you understand the strategic goals for this book and the theories behind my approach.

The topics to be discussed in this chapter are:

1. My definition of the disease
2. Ultimate objective of the book

3. The chronic problem
4. My background and clinical perspective

My definition of the disease

Within the medical community, there is a longstanding debate over an agreed-upon definition of *disease*. The World Health Organization does not define disease, but rather defines *health* as "a complete state of physical, mental, and social well-being and not merely the absence of infirmity." On the other hand, the American Psychological Association defines *disease* as "a definite pathological process with organic origins, marked by a characteristic set of symptoms that may affect the entire body or a part of the body, impairing functioning."

According to Merriam-Webster, *disease* is "a condition of a living animal or plant body which impairs normal functioning and is manifested by distinguishing signs and symptoms." More obvious and well-known examples are heart disease, diabetes, Alzheimer's disease, depression, and substance use disorders.

In addition to these definitions, I also define a *disease* as "any chronic entity causing persistent impairment in one or more areas of a person's life (e.g., mental, physical, or social)." Some examples of a disease under this definition could include selfishness, racism, resentments, over-working, under-working, poor communication skills, materialism, or any one of the Seven Deadly Sins (pride, greed, lust, envy, gluttony, wrath, sloth). In the Anonymous arena (e.g., Alcoholics Anonymous or AA), a commonly cited definition members use is that *disease* means "not at ease." If there is an aspect of life that continually presents challenges, and a person struggles to lessen or manage it, that is their "disease."

Therefore, I believe everyone has their own variation of a disease, as we all have areas of struggle. And we might also employ some type of recovery (a plan for healthier results or outcomes) to manage our diseases.

When we've lived with a disease for some time, it can feel like we're struggling against a conscious, determined entity with human-like attributes. Our job is to recognize its patterns, strengths, and weaknesses in order to devise a plan to manage or lessen its impact. If disease is a relentless adversary or opponent, we need to respect its capabilities and work diligently to avoid being weakened by it. In later chapters, I'll discuss some attributes of the disease in this context, as well as how to disempower and manage this type of human-like entity.

Ultimate objective of the book

To win the battle!

This strategy guide is for families battling the diseases of mental illness and substance abuse who may feel they have tried everything but are not willing to give up the fight.

This book provides the knowledge and skills I've deemed critical after countless hours working with families to navigate pre-treatment and prepare for a lifetime of healthy recovery, finally putting an end to the perpetual tug-of-war of trying to get your family member help. However, the guide is not meant to serve as a comprehensive catalog of every substance abuse disorder, nor is it a deep dive into psychiatric conditions. You won't be inundated with statistics and medical terminologies. The book isn't a diagnostic tool, a specific clinical recommendation, or the end-all to treating substance use disorder and/or mental illness. Rather, my book is designed to impart what I believe is the most critical information and the necessary skill set proven effective in my collaboration with thousands of family members in acute crisis. The goal is to get your family members help, no matter their mental health condition or substance of abuse.

Please note, though this book is mainly intended for the families of struggling loved ones, this guide can also be utilized as a reference when your loved one has attained a level of healthy functioning (e.g., after completing treatment). For example, the chapters that speak to traits consistent with a strong recovery program, ways to maintain long-term recovery, healthy communications skills, and the attributes of a healthy fellowship are discussions that can enhance a healthy path of living. Also, if your loved one needs to help a struggling person in the future, they can refer to this guide to pay it forward.

When I refer to families, I am not limiting the discussion to biological, chosen, or immediate family. This book can also be useful for cousins, relatives, romantic partners, friends, teammates, teachers, coaches, co-workers—any individual who is part of the person's support system and wants to advocate for getting them help.

Last, it is common knowledge that mental health can use much more acknowledgement, financial support, policy improvements, and recognition at the social justice level. The process of getting your loved one help can be even more difficult if inadequate resources or limited accessibility to services present as obstacles. I believe it is a very important issue to address, but it is beyond the scope of this book. This book is focused on aspects people can control within the family and at the individual levels. As a community, I encourage all of us to be proponents of mental health policy enhancement. So, please get involved in any way you can. Helping your family and loved one can be the first step.

The chronic problem

- ✓ Too much of the *what* and not enough of the *how*
- ✓ What about other, co-occurring mental health conditions?

The most common complaints families express to me, whether it's in my private practice, during family support groups, at a local church or community center, or when I'm supporting the family system in treatment, all seem to follow a theme—the need for actual strategies to get family members into treatment and keep them on a path of recovery.

When families speak to a treatment center's admissions representative or come home from a mental health conference with an armful of pamphlets, they are hoping to find strategies to get their family member into treatment. Repeatedly, they are let down. Most recommendations are surface level. Pamphlets are littered with proverbial, well-intended advice such as "Get them into treatment," "Set boundaries," or "Show them tough love." But these suggestions fall short of explaining exactly *how to* organize, plan, and execute these interventions.

Certainly, you can find helpful books and online advice, but many are focused on substance abuse and don't encompass the comorbidity with other mental health conditions (e.g., bipolar disorder, schizophrenia, depression, panic attacks, post-traumatic stress disorder (PTSD), suicidality, etc.). Similarly, hiring an interventionist may yield results but can be limited in scope if the intervention targets the person's struggles with substances and doesn't take into account other co-occurring psychiatric conditions. One of the most common statements I've heard from family members after working with some variation of a team is that the intervention was great for addressing the alcohol or substance use, but didn't tackle critical areas such as suicidal thoughts, manic episodes, and psychosis. On the other hand, family members may only focus on the mental health condition and avoid addressing the substance use issue, because they feel their loved one's use isn't excessive or problematic (e.g., a person with bipolar disorder who smokes moderate amounts of marijuana three to four days per week to help with sleep, or a person with depression who binge drinks alcohol only on the weekends to unwind from work).

Figure 1. shows the various types of approaches families often find limited in meeting their affected loved ones' needs. Instead, I use a comprehensive approach when working with families to strategize a plan.

Figure 1. Various Approaches to Working with Families

Rationale for my comprehensive approach

It is important to note that both mental health disorders (e.g., major depressive disorder, bipolar disorder, schizophrenia, post-traumatic stress disorder, etc.) and substance abuse disorders (alcohol abuse, marijuana dependence, methamphetamine use disorder, etc.) are identified in the *Diagnostic Statistical Manual-V (DSM-5)* as psychiatric conditions. Please note, the *DSM-5* is a manual used by mental health professionals for assessment and diagnosis of mental health disorders. Though mental health conditions and substance abuse disorders are both psychiatric issues, they are treated separately in this book because, generally speaking, many people in the community not as familiar or educated about mental health view them as mutually exclusive, or independent entities. Based on the many cases I have treated, I would certainly classify both under the umbrella of psychiatric conditions as the *DSM-5* does and have found they consistently interrelate and overlap in many ways.

For instance, a person struggling with severe anxiety may smoke methamphetamines to help alleviate excessive worry. However, prolonged and increased use of this substance can worsen anxiety by disrupting sleep and stimulating racing thoughts. Is the person smoking methamphetamines to alleviate anxiety, or are methamphetamines causing the person to feel anxious? The question of what came first—the chicken or the egg—doesn't matter at this juncture of someone's struggle. Both problems need to be addressed.

My comprehensive approach includes mental health especially when substance abuse is involved because, in my experience, substance use disorder is not a stand-alone condition. Sometimes, clients and family members state, "My only issue is alcohol," "My son is a substance-only case," or, "Our daughter just needs to work on her meth addiction." Truthfully, I have never worked with a client with a chronic substance issue (or some other form of addiction such as excessive eating, sex, gambling, etc.), who did not have a mental or emotional health condition as a co-occurring issue. In the case of most chronic abuse, the substance has served as a sophisticated coping tool for some aspect of a person's life that is causing distress. This can be a medical disorder, psychiatric condition, difficulty regulating emotions, unhealthy thought patterns, a past/recent trauma, or a current stressor—all of these examples fall under the umbrella of mental or emotional health. Sometimes, clients will state, "I've never been diagnosed with a mental health disorder," or family members may tell me, "We looked online, and she does not meet the criteria for depression/anxiety/post-traumatic stress disorder, etc." It's important to note that when someone has not been professionally diagnosed with a mental health condition or does not meet the full criteria for a psychiatric disorder, it doesn't eliminate the possibility that mental or emotional issues are contributing to or causing their struggle with substance abuse.

Alternately, a client may have mental health issues and no problem with substances. These clients still fall under a risk factor umbrella. If their mental health struggles are not managed, they are at risk of turning to substances as a means of achieving relief. Family members have stated, "Our son has never abused substances," "Our daughter will never abuse substances because her mom was an addict," or, "My husband is very religious and won't touch substances." I caution these family members that if their loved ones struggle with a mental health condition, they carry an increased risk for using substances to cope. Also, family members might later discover their loved ones have been secretly abusing substances or engaging in other unhealthy behaviors, such as excessive eating, spending, gambling, sex, etc.

It is highly recommended that your family member seeks professional advice (e.g., psychiatrist, psychologist, therapist, clinical social worker, school counselor, etc.) for a reliable diagnosis. Self-evaluation or online tests are not valid methods of attaining an accurate diagnosis. A professional is trained to ask subjective and qualitative questions, and to integrate the answers into an assessment. Using an interview format, they may also capture other important information such as the severity of one's condition, risk factors, strengths, and protective elements. Sometimes a person may withhold some facts, minimize symptoms, or be unaware that a symptom is problematic, which is why having a family member present at appointments is optimal if your loved one consents. Additionally, a mental health professional may also integrate quantitative measures such as empirically validated instruments and psychometric test batteries to supplement data for a more accurate and comprehensive diagnosis.

It is also important to note that this strategy guide addresses the need to recognize and validate the psychiatric aspect of a person struggling; however, it will not distinctly provide interventions for specific mental health conditions (e.g., schizophrenia, bipolar disorder, post-traumatic stress disorder, etc.). In other words, statements such as "This is how you talk to someone with schizophrenia/social anxiety/ major depressive disorder" as well as detailed steps for engaging someone going through an active manic episode, experiencing a psychotic event or acute stress, etc. are beyond the breadth of this book. Yet some of the interventions in this guide are general in focus and can be implemented across specific psychiatric conditions. For example, tools such as active listening, validation, empathy, and healthy boundary setting can be utilized with a loved one having paranoia due to excessive marijuana use, feeling agitated due to heightened depression, or experiencing worry due to a crisis. If you feel your family needs particular interventions and tools based on your loved one's distinct condition, please contact a medical or health care professional experienced in treating those conditions.

Urgency and gap in knowledge

Often, I'm invited to give talks in collaboration with other mental health professionals. My designated counterparts will touch upon important topics related to mental health disorders—psychiatric medications, neurotransmitters, treatment approaches, and so on, while I discuss the dark, manipulative sides of disease (e.g., manipulation, dishonesty, denial, avoidance, blame, minimization, etc.), how to devise strategies to fight against it, and tools to get a struggling loved one help. During the Q & A portion, most questions come from desperate family members seeking advice and direction to save significant people in their lives.

Based on what I hear in family interviews, or when I see countless tragedies due to mental health and substance abuse in the news, or when I come across articles about people trying to manage care for a mentally ill family member, the shared reality is that families in our communities are struggling and reaching a point of hopelessness. There is no shortage of literature about mental health conditions and drugs, no lack of treatment centers for almost any substance abuse or psychiatric condition at nearly every acuity (intensity/degree) level. But the quagmire families continually express is that knowledge and available resources do not necessarily result in recovery. Often, they have read extensively about the disorders; in fact, some may feel they know more than the clinician at times. They understand the dangerous effects of illicit substance use and have identified three to five potential places for treatment, but the questions remain. They tell me, "We have book knowledge, resources, and treatment centers on standby, but we don't know how to formulate everything into a plan. We still live in fear that our loved one will die or harm one of us. How do we use the information to get them into treatment?"

Facing this scenario on a weekly basis for almost two decades has led me to recognize the huge gaps between knowledge and the skills needed to get family members help. People may attain advice from a clinician, gain insight from a support group, or seek the guidance of an interventionist, but what they need is an actual, step-by-step guide, a *How To* for battling the diseases of substance abuse and mental illness with the end goal of getting unwell family members help. This is why I consolidated everything I've been teaching families for years into a strategic, easy-to-read manual. I am hoping this book can be an important weapon in the fight against these diseases; a tool that helps families win not only the current battle, but eventually the war.

My background and clinical perspective

My clinical approach to taking on the diseases of mental illness and substance abuse is similar to a battle, but the process of staying healthy does not have to feel like an endless war. I view the disease as the antagonist in the fight, and recovery is the best defense *and* offense against it. Indeed, the early stages of the recovery process will present some fierce battles. The disease can seem like a separate, intelligent entity, constantly jockeying for position and changing its game to survive. Our task is to adapt and strategize to limit its capabilities. It's no different than combating a troublesome personality trait, a newly diagnosed genetic disorder, a self-defeating thought pattern, a chronic medical condition, or a novel virus. Each requires an active, diligent, and responsive strategy.

Personifying these diseases doesn't mean I'm taking overall accountability away from your struggling family member or claiming that their impairment, actions, or struggles can be solely blamed on the disease. But by identifying this entity as separate from your family member, by making it concrete and attempting to understand the way it operates, we will be better equipped to devise a strategy to battle it. You know that beneath the unhealthiness, chaos, and dysfunction of the disease, your loved ones are smart, loving, funny, compassionate, talented, and special individuals worth every ounce of fight you can muster.

Don't be intimidated. This battle won't always be an unending dog fight. Managing the diseases of mental illness and substance abuse is quite possible, and people in recovery can lead healthy, productive, and rewarding lives. My suggested approach is not vastly different from what a patient would do to manage diabetes or an immune deficiency disorder. What is needed is an evolving game plan to keep the disease at bay. My "25 Must Knows" and the strategies in this guide are the foundational knowledge for families to get loved ones onto a healthy path where treatment is the ONLY option.

So, why the fight? Some insight into my approach

Before discussing my personal fight, it is important to state that my challenges may pale in comparison to what your loved ones are enduring. I recognize the gravity of complicated trauma, immense grief and loss, and chronic substance abuse. However, my intention is to demonstrate the common thread we all share; we need to overcome our mental battles no matter what challenge we are facing.

The battle-ready lens through which I see the diseases of mental illness and substance abuse comes from the fight or flight impulse instilled in me growing up. I had to fight for many things, and my ability to flourish didn't always come easily. Unfortunately, there were occasions when I abandoned the fight and took the flight route. My personal fights weren't due to challenging family members or any particular dysfunction; in fact, I am humbly grateful for a nurturing family who provided unconditional acceptance and many opportunities to be successful. But while reflecting on the research of Erik Erikson, a psychologist who developed one of the most impactful theories about the stages of development, I realized the detours and obstacles I encountered were due to bouts of self-doubt and lack of direction—my own version of disease.

Though I encountered my share of verbal and physical bullying as well as discrimination in my childhood and young adult years, my fighter mentality mainly arose in response to academic challenges, which had a deeper emotional impact for me. During my early school days, I experienced some success but also rough patches, especially in my younger adulthood when it was time to grow up and address that quintessential Thanksgiving-dinnertime question, "What do you want to be when you grow up?" And in college, after several trips to the dean's office to fill out a form to change my major, I finally graduated in six-and-a-half years (yes, just one semester less than it took Chris Farley's character in *Tommy Boy*). A failed stint in medical school followed, then a psychology PhD program that ended prematurely. Leapfrogging across several jobs, I realized I was in a fight with myself. Although there were times I took flight, I never gave up on the journey. After navigating the unpredictable waters of wavering self-assurance and countless nights praying to my higher power for guidance, I finally set my compass on a path I had known deep down I should pursue all along—being of service to others. My mom always told me I had these gifts: empathy, compassion, the ability to read people's emotions, a disarming personality, and the skill of choosing words to make others feel better. Let me tell you, at times I felt lost and hopeless, and wanted to get up and run far away. Now, I want to reach out to others who also are feeling exasperated and without a glimmer of hope.

Although I always sensed a bigger purpose, I hadn't been able to find the right dart to stick. Everything changed for me after an emotional one-on-one conversation with Dr. Michael Mumford, my major advisor in my first PhD program and the person who solidified my realization that I had embarked upon the wrong graduate program in psychology. He encouraged and granted me the permission to transfer to the counseling program and pursue my true calling (Thank you, Dr. Mumford, for that life-changing conversation.). Little did I know, my calling was waiting for me just one building and department over. Now, I'm grateful to be in a field that aligns with my values and principles and utilizes my skill set. Each day, I have the opportunity to instill hope in the same way hope was restored in me. I'm where I am supposed to be, striving to make an impact with those struggling with mental health. I get up each morning absolutely fulfilled by my professional calling, while pushing myself to be even one scintilla better than the day before. And I have an insatiable hunger to keep getting better at what I do.

Through academic battles, my fighter approach developed, but there was another source—the athletic opportunities provided by those same, selfless parents who sacrificed so much for me. Thankfully, sports came much more easily to me. As a child, I competed in combat karate tournaments and did well, winning a few trophies taller than I was. As a junior tennis player, I earned a state and western national ranking. In college, as a founding father of my fraternity, I played intramural sports, helping our organization attain various awards. And these days, I compete at the world level in Brazilian Jiu-Jitsu, a ground-fighting/grappling martial art involving submission tactics. Now, I realize the lessons from honing a competitive mindset weren't so much about achieving that gold medal, trophy, or ranking, but rather about appreciating the importance of the process. Even after my failed attempts at medical school and another PhD program, I didn't realize until later how much I had gained from those tough processes—invaluable insights about myself and my purpose.

Some of the most illuminating lessons about myself and life are learned during arduous training sessions on the Jiu-Jitsu mats. I am constantly pushed to my outer limits, forced to look for new solutions based on narrowing choices, leveraged into uncomfortable positions, and compelled to keep fighting until the clock sounds or the instructor says it's time. When I push myself beyond my perceived threshold of comfort, I've discovered things aren't so hard the next time around. As world-renowned, motivational speaker Les Brown once said, "When you do things in life that are easy, life will be hard; when you do things in life that are hard, life will be easy."

Participating in competitive sports have contributed to my "fighter approach."

One major lesson I've learned on my Jiu-Jitsu journey is that it's never okay to mentally tap out, no matter how desperate I become. When I reach a point where I want to give up, that's the defining moment when salient lessons are learned, and the biggest growth spurts occur. Whenever situations seem unbearably painful—emotionally and mentally—I remind myself to push past what seems to be a breaking point. And somehow, I'm able to push myself to new limits.

Similarly, the everyday adversaries of substance abuse and mental illness push a person to their limits. Yet, like my Jiu-Jitsu opponents, the disease is not the true challenge. The biggest opponent for all of us, really, is the person in the mirror and the thoughts telling us to tap out. We have to stay in the fight.

Several times in my life, I was ready to tap out, give up the fight, and, as a result, leave my potential unfulfilled. But each time I found myself falling, wandering aimlessly on the brink of succumbing to a ten count, I summoned the fighter deep within and stood back up on life's canvas. Every time I struggled to my feet, a part of me felt more resilient, with a slightly clearer vision. Actor and speaker Denzel Washington wisely said, "If you're going to fall, fall forward." And motivational speaker Les Brown believes, "If you fall, fall on your back. If you can look up, you can get back up." These are two very successful men who have fallen throughout their lives but continue to take on the fight, never giving up on themselves or others.

Lastly, the mindset I adopted to fight through my failures is the same strategy families and clients can use to persevere through their own struggles. Instead of calling them "failures," I'd rather define these moments of adversity as life's setbacks—events that knock a person off course. People who are chronically struggling sometimes view a setback as a failure, deficiency, or a missed opportunity. In his article, "Treat Failure Like a Scientist," author James Clear claims failures are simply instructive data points we can learn from. This data is inputted into our mental compass, allowing us to navigate back onto our intended path. True lessons are learned on the journey to right ourselves. Clear's thinking aligns with my own beliefs, that people who stay in the fight view a setback as a golden opportunity for growth.

What I have learned through my own internal struggles and by listening to these leaders and many others is that our fights can look different in some ways and similar in many others. However, we all share attributes we can summon to keep us in the fight—grit and resilience. I truly believe every single human on this earth—child or adult—has these inherent qualities, deep down, no matter our circumstances, conditions, or past experiences. This includes your family members struggling with substance use and mental illness, no matter how hopeless or against the ropes they may be.

The epitome of hope—a life-changing case story

One of my most unforgettable and gratifying cases was a gentleman named Matthew. Our work together exemplified it all—desperation, fight, and eventually, success. He has graciously allowed me to share his story in the hopes of helping others who are feeling demoralized or believe tapping out is the only option left.

Several years ago, *The Doctors* television show invited me to be a part of Matthew's treatment team. Matthew was six-foot-two and athletic, an avid skateboarder and driven snowboarder with national, commercial sponsors. He had engaged in various competitive sports throughout his life. As a young adult, he'd been diagnosed with cancer and prescribed medication to assist with the debilitating pain from the treatment. When the painkillers weren't "doing the trick" any longer, he transitioned to heroin, which was more accessible and numbed the pain equally well. After a family fallout, legal issues led to a downward spiral. Matthew decided to enter treatment and try to get sober. At the time, he was not truly committed to changing. After three months of treatment, he found himself once again in a dark place. Without the direction of a foreseeable future and experiencing increasing hopelessness, he relapsed on heroin. One fateful night, his life was utterly altered.

Matthew awoke in a hospital bed and was informed that both legs had been amputated. After a heroin binge, he had spent nearly twenty hours unconscious and in a contorted position that had severely diminished blood circulation to his legs. Overnight, his life changed irrevocably.

But Matthew was a fighter. His involvement in a lifetime of competitive athletics and a family who refused to give up, created in him the relentless fight necessary to claw back onto a healthy life path. In therapy, Matthew and I worked on reframing any unhealthy belief systems as a result of the tragic event (e.g., overwhelming self-guilt, internal anger, and emotional pain he caused his family), attain healthier ways to cope (e.g., daily sobriety goals, social engagement, physical exercise, healthy diet, stress management, self-soothing skills), and instilling hope (e.g., self-forgiveness, goal-setting, and self-acceptance). He realized that lamenting the past would only keep him stuck, impeding any forward momentum. Matthew was determined to work diligently in each session and left our meetings with a renewed belief in a promising tomorrow.

Although it took diligent work, Matthew re-established his path and elevated the game plan of his life to a new level. Through his dedicated efforts in physical rehabilitation for strength training and conditioning, in individual counseling to deal with grief and loss as well as addiction, and during countless medical appointments for pain management, he was able to make remarkable breakthroughs and finally fracture dysfunctional patterns of thinking and behaving.

Four years later, Matthew started water skiing and reconnected with one of the loves of his life—the snow. Now, he's a highly accomplished slalom skier. His ultimate goal is to compete in the National Championships and Paralympics. Matthew embodies a fighter, someone who, in the depths of darkness, conjured up grit and never gave up on himself or his loved ones. He had every reason to tap out; instead, he tapped into the fighting spirit that had been in him all along.

Caption: Matthew on The Doctors show, snow skiing and waterskiing.

Many of the families I've encountered feel they have no more to give after many trials. They, too, can find the strength to get up again. My role has always been to guide these families of fighters through the flames of failure with a clear purpose and intention. In the same way I (and many others) were part of Matthew's road to recovery, I aspire to do the same for your families.

With that said, if you're not ready to tap out and you still have the resolve to take on the disease, let us begin preparing for the fight.

Chapter 2
Key Book Notes

This chapter is designed to help you better understand the book's important considerations, terminologies, and my writing style. The following topics will be addressed in this chapter:

1. Targeted families
2. Pre-treatment and treatment (recovery)
3. Cultural considerations
4. Age considerations
5. Use of statistics and content validity

Targeted families: Adults nearing crisis or in crisis (but others can still benefit)

Please take note that this guide is predominantly focused on strategies to get a loved one into the first phase of treatment. These individuals are typically nearing imminent crisis levels if they do not get some form of treatment soon; most likely, they are refusing any kind of help. Though this book may touch upon elements needed on both the individual and family levels once a loved one is in treatment, this guide does not delve into specific treatment modalities (e.g.,

Strength-Based Therapy, Emotion-Focused Therapy, Psychodynamic Approach, Solution-Focused Therapy, Neurodivergent Therapy, etc.). Consult with your therapist or appropriate professional for guidance on these various treatment approaches.

That said, it is important to start by discussing how *crisis* is defined in this book. In this guide, crisis can be viewed on a spectrum ranging from developing crisis (low end) to imminent crisis (high end). Generally speaking, people are deemed to be in a state of developing crisis when they are in potential danger of harming themselves, harming others, or when they are moving towards being gravely disabled and requiring help sooner rather than later. Please note, *gravely disabled* means that a person cannot care for their own basic needs pertaining to food, shelter, and self-care and will experience deleterious consequences (e.g., potential death) if they do not attain assistance. However, people in imminent crisis need *immediate* medical or mental health attention because of the very high likelihood of danger (e.g., survived a suicide attempt or has desire, intent, and means to harm self, experiencing a psychotic episode, harmed others, or has desire, intent, and means to harm others, etc.). If your loved one is in imminent danger, stop here and call 911 immediately for assistance.

The knowledge and strategies in this book can still have utility for loved ones in imminent crisis, especially if they continue to deny help or refuse the medical attention necessary at this level of danger. However, this book was created primarily for those families who feel they have a member in developing-to-mid-range levels of crises, and if that member doesn't get help soon and they stay unhealthy, it could lead to an imminent crisis state. The intended audience for this guide is families on the brink of throwing in the towel after trying to help their adult-aged loved one struggling with a mental health or substance use issue. It is for those families who feel they've exhausted all options and need strategies quickly, families who fear their family member may lose their life, harm someone, or put themself in grave danger if help is not received. For families at this level of acuity, the unwell members are rapidly moving towards a point of needing a higher level of care—such as inpatient hospitalization or residential treatment.

Yet, families with loved ones in a very low degree of *struggle* (not yet crisis level) can also benefit from the knowledge and tools in this guide. Those struggling with mental health and/or substance use at a low level of dysfunction have not necessarily reached a level of desperation or crisis. They may be stuck in what Prochaska and DiClemente, the researchers who created the Stages of Change model, call the Precontemplation ("I don't realize there's a problem") or Contemplation Stages ("I realize there is a problem but unsure if I want to change, do something about it, or know how to change"). People in this lower range of struggle have not reached the point where the world is crumbling around them. They may still have options and resources or believe their lifestyle is not detrimental enough to require change. But they can reach a crisis level in a matter of time if they do not make healthy changes and their issues begin to compound.

As a general reference, low-to-moderate levels of *struggle* could mean a person is still able to function somewhat effectively in certain areas of their lives and hasn't entered a crisis state (developing, midrange, or imminent) yet. Their conditions are problematic but haven't caused significant impairment. For instance, people struggling with a moderate level of depression, anxiety, or substance abuse disorder may still be able to adequately perform job functions, maintain personal relationships, and take care of basic needs, but their conditions may limit their full potential or create obstacles in their progress. In other words, they tend to have enough gas in the tank to continue traveling along in their current state. However, if they continue engaging in the same lifestyle, they will accelerate to a crisis point eventually, due to the progressive nature of the disease.

People at a more severe level of struggle are most likely at the fringe or already entering a crisis state, almost fully impaired and typically, not able to function in most—if not all—areas of their lives. For instance, people in a severe state of depression cannot hold down a job, stay isolated from others, refuse help, cannot care for their basic needs of food/shelter/hygiene, and may require hospitalization or intensive treatment to move towards a healthier baseline level of functioning. Potential outcomes for those who remain in this mode can be harm to self or others, the triggering of psychotic breaks, drug overdoses, jail time, or involuntary institutionalization.

An important aspect to touch upon here is the notion of complete abstinence from all mind-altering, non-prescribed substances (e.g., alcohol, marijuana, benzodiazepines, etc.) when developing the treatment plan for a person in crisis. The question is whether or not complete abstinence is the only way or whether using substances "manageably" is a viable alternative of lessening harm. Harm reduction, when pertaining to substance use, is a treatment approach that views the use of certain substances, the frequency of use, and the amount of substance used as potentially less critical than the other issues a person may be navigating through (e.g., acute trauma, intense physical pain, unbearable grief). A harm reduction approach suggests responsible, managed use of substances to help mitigate the more severe symptoms a person is going through. I will further discuss the idea of harm reduction and complete abstinence in Chapter 6.

Summary Crisis Guide

- Gravely disabled or imminent (high end crisis)—Requires immediate help (e.g., hospitalization, intensive treatment). Likely need to call 911.
- Developing (low end crisis) to mid-range (moderate crisis)— Moving towards imminent crisis if person does not receive help. This is the target population for this book.

Pre-treatment (aka Pre-treatment Zone) and treatment (recovery)

As mentioned earlier, this book is largely focused on assisting families in what I call the Pre-treatment Zone. In the Pre-treatment Zone, families are desperate to get their loved ones—who have been refusing help—into treatment. If the situation persists, the family feels that deleterious consequences may be around the corner. The support system in the Pre-treatment Zone is experiencing intense fear, anxiety, loss, confusion, and desperation. They may believe their loved one is no longer able to care for their basic needs adequately and might be in danger of harming self or others. They probably believe intensive care or interventions are necessary to avoid detrimental consequences.

Figure 2 represents an abbreviated portion of the Phases of Recovery Model that will be fully addressed in Chapter 7. As I mentioned, a major gap exists for providing families with the strategies needed to make the jump from the Pre-treatment Zone to Phase 1, the first thirty to ninety days of treatment. This book will help families fill that gap.

<table>
<tr><td>**Pre-treatment Zone**</td><td>**Phase 1
30-90 days (ICU)**</td></tr>
<tr><td>*(Time period prior to loved one
getting help or treatment)*</td><td>*High rate of struggle
(relapse and lapse)*</td></tr>
</table>

Figure 2. Phases of Recovery—
Pre-treatment Zone and Phase 1 only

Phase 1 begins when a person is receiving help, and a treatment plan has been implemented. However, Phase 1 can also be viewed similarly to the Intensive Care Unit (ICU), as people at this juncture need to address more critical-level needs (e.g., recovering from a suicide attempt or drug overdose, stabilizing from a psychotic episode, treating acute trauma, etc.). Often, families who reach out to me are in a state of extreme desperation. They may have tried a lower-level treatment route that consisted of seeing an individual therapist on an outpatient basis, utilizing psychiatric services monthly, or attending a support group. But now, their struggles have heightened, these levels of interventions are no longer working, and a higher level of care is needed. Examples of higher-level care include a detoxification facility, inpatient treatment, or a residential treatment program—all provide a high degree of oversight and accountability. A higher level of care also means removal from immediate environments that may be contributing to the chronic problem. This is a critical aspect with patients at a heightened acuity level; often, surroundings can present problematic dynamics. Some examples of counterproductive environments are highly distressing jobs, dysfunctional family dynamics, unhealthy peers who abuse substances, homes that provide isolation and avoidance, friends or family who enable an unhealthy lifestyle, etc.

So, how is recovery defined? The first question that usually comes to mind when recovery is mentioned is, "Which substance is the problem?" While it may be true that recovery can refer to someone working to stay sober, the term is more expansive than that. According to the Substance Abuse and Mental Health Services Administration (SAMHSA), recovery is "a process of change through which individuals improve their health and wellness, live a self-directed life, and strive to reach their full potential." It involves having a plan in place for healthier outcomes or a return to a baseline level of functioning. It's similar to treatment in terms of the end goal (e.g., sobriety and effective mental health management). Treatment is typically the actual process of receiving assistance (e.g., inpatient, residential, partial hospitalization, outpatient services, individual therapy, etc.), while recovery is the overall journey of maintaining a healthier lifestyle, beyond—and usually, as a result of some form of treatment.

Within the recovery framework, I believe each one of us are on some path toward healthier living. We can be in recovery from a job loss, medical condition, relationship breakup, major change of lifestyle due to a pandemic, death of a family member, kids leaving home for college, and so on. In order to get through these challenges, we need to create a path to recovery and maintain it to ensure the issue does not become chronic and problematic.

Here's an example I use to illustrate the importance of a recovery program, and how it extends beyond mental health and substance abuse. Let's say a patient sees a physician for a general check-up and is found to have high blood pressure and a strong family history of this condition. The patient is then assigned a diagnosis of hypertension. The doctor and patient discuss a treatment plan consisting of hypertension medications, lessening cigarette smoking, lowering sodium intake, increasing physical exercise to four times a week, and engaging in meditation techniques to lower stress. If the patient returns to the doctor's office four months later and has a normal blood pressure, does that mean the patient can go back to that old lifestyle? Not if they want to stay healthy! They will always need to adhere to the recovery plan, being respectful of the capabilities of the hypertension condition (which I will call the "disease"). Earlier, I likened a disease to any entity that causes challenges and impairments in our lives and needs to be managed. Therefore, we all have our own versions of diseases we navigate throughout our lifetime.

Cultural considerations

According to Merriam-Webster Dictionary, *culture* is the "customary beliefs, social norms, and material traits of a racial, religious, or social group." During a community presentation, an audience member asked whether different cultures are taken into account when strategizing with families. It's a valid and important question. Certainly, there are varying cultural considerations when working directly with families (e.g., communication patterns, familial structure, gender roles, birth-order responsibilities, etc.), but my consistent response never changes. These tools are designed to fight the disease on a broadband level, and the family's cultural or ethnic heritage doesn't matter; the disease does not discriminate by race, age, sexual orientation, gender, culture, socio-economic status, religion, philosophy, or religious beliefs. Most often, the symptomologies of depression and suicidality (e.g., isolation, intense sadness, and hopelessness) will look similar, making the knowledge and tools I teach relevant across cultures as well.

In my practice, I have worked with families across many ethnicities, including Asian, Middle Eastern, European, and African American—and let me tell you, it's the same disease no matter what part of the world your family originated from. The disease's manifestations may vary in presentation from individual to individual, and symptoms may express slightly differently across ethnicities and cultures, but its unwavering purpose is to isolate, replicate, and impair, no matter what.

Stigma

However, there are some important and specific aspects of culture that can create obstacles in getting a loved one help. First, stigma regarding mental health and substance addiction can serve as a major impediment for individuals and family members. According to Oxford Languages, *stigma* is "a mark of disgrace associated with a particular circumstance, quality, or person." In the various work I do with families and the community, much of the stigma regarding addiction and mental health stems from a lack of education, misinformation, prejudice, or erroneous assumptions. For instance, there is a common belief among people not educated on substance addiction that people can *will* themselves to stop. They do not realize those chronically struggling have both a mental and physical dependence and need a support team. Along similar lines, a large faction of people strongly believe that conditions such as depression and anxiety are largely self-induced and, again, that people can easily control their negative or worrisome thought patterns by simply adopting positive thinking habits. Yes, creating more positive beliefs is an important aspect in therapy, but it is not the only way. When struggles are chronic and severe, it takes collaboration, guidance, and support.

In some cultures across the world, a strong negative attitude exists regarding people who struggle with mental illness (some cultures more severe than others); these prejudices can prevent people from getting help due to societal and internal shame. A family might worry about exposing personal struggles and decide to keep it within the home. Some cultures believe a decline in mental health is due to mystical reasons, caused by bad deeds committed by the person struggling as a form of punishment. Also, mental health and substance addiction can be viewed as an internal weakness or character flaw, and a family may avoid exposing a loved one's "weakness" which can render the family unit vulnerable or incapable of solving their own problems.

These types of stigmas can be very dangerous, leading people to feel helpless. An example of how a specific cultural belief can serve as an impediment to getting help took place in a support group I facilitated. An Asian male sought help for his older brother, who was having extreme, angry outbursts coupled with severe depression. For the past year, he had been verbally abusive to their elderly mother, with whom he resided. The younger brother stated that his sibling refused to get help, and their mother was afraid of him. I asked whether he was willing to talk to his brother about his concerns and recommend getting help. Wide-eyed, he responded that in his Asian culture, "We never confront our elders, as it will be seen as an attempt to shame." He also mentioned that his culture did not look well upon mental illness, and "people tend to hide it to avoid humiliation."

I told him I completely understood and supported his cultural beliefs but was concerned the same beliefs may be putting his mother in danger. And without some treatment, his brother may get worse. After exploring different options with him, the main priority remained—the need to talk to his brother. There were no other family members who would step in. He thanked me politely for my time, and he never returned to the support group. I often wondered about what happened with his family situation.

On a more positive note, what we are finding is that the more people talk openly about mental health and addiction, the less stigma is attached. This waning of stigma is exponentially impactful when a person shares their own struggles. Countless times, I have seen that when a member in my group therapy session shares an intimate detail about their life (e.g., past sexual abuse, suicidal tendencies/attempts, depression regarding sexuality, etc.), other members will share more openly about their own traumas. Sharing gives others permission to feel safe to also do so; it validates their own experiences and normalizes the struggle. Open sharing of struggles can have a larger, positive impact and a de-stigmatization effect when the person is considered high profile (e.g., actor, professional athlete, political leader, celebrity, wealthy or powerful individual, etc.). We sometimes live under the false assumption that people who have attained a high degree of success are beyond human and do not have struggles like everyone else. When these more recognized individuals share intimate details of their struggles, it humanizes them and reminds us that they are ordinary people with vulnerabilities. Taking these people down from an unrealistic pedestal weakens the stigma.

Lastly, we are starting to see the stigma of mental illness wearing away on a global level, as younger generations are talking more freely and openly about their struggles via social media, songs, talks, speeches, etc. We are also seeing other countries committing more resources and programs towards mental health issues. Over the past ten years and counting, my clientele has become more ethnically and culturally diverse (i.e., age, gender, gender identity, professions)—in individual therapy, residential treatment, and support groups. Cultures historically resistant to seeking mental health support are increasingly matriculating into programs specifically for mental health and substance addiction support.

We are nowhere near the level we need to be to erase the stigma, but we are definitely making incremental progress towards lessening its impact. Hopefully, as we talk more openly about our own struggles and witness treatment successes, leaders can recognize the important effects treating mental illness can have on communities, the nation, and the world as a whole.

It's important to remember that this book is mostly geared toward family members seeking help getting an intimate loved one into treatment, and they will ultimately have a better understanding of their family's cultural norms based on ethnic background, customs, religious beliefs, communication patterns, language, etc. But families should also recognize that subcultures may be part of their loved one's life experience. For instance, a family may have a hard time connecting with a son due to a lack of understanding regarding his recent identification as transgender. The inability to comprehend this facet would create tension, and the son could feel isolated and alone. Below, I will talk about two critical concepts creating deeper interpersonal connection by way of better understanding cultures.

Cultural humility and competence

Cultural humility is allowing healthy dialogue to try to understand another's identifications as they pertain to ethnicity, race, gender, gender identity, sexual orientation, socioeconomic status, education, belief systems, religious orientations, political affiliations, etc. *Cultural competency* is reaching an understanding about the "way of life" of a group based on norms, customs, and beliefs. These two major areas need to be attended to when building trust with your loved one. If a lack of familiarity with the struggling loved one's cultural beliefs is causing problems, the family unit needs to take responsibility and work on it. I call this notion *shared family accountability*. Note: having cultural humility and competency doesn't require agreement with a person's cultural beliefs, but rather a level of understanding and acceptance in order to interact more effectively—essentially, having a deeper connection with others. For instance, if a family is willing to authentically understand a person's identification as bisexual, this interrelation will help the person feel less alienated and more willing to trust members. Even if the other members may not agree with this lifestyle as it may be contrary to their belief system, they are willing to work towards a level of acceptance as a group. In this way, the loved one can feel that the family truly wants what is best, and this instills a greater sense of trust. On the other hand, if a group is resistant to cultural humility and competence, it will be much harder to gain the trust of the loved one needing help. They will be less likely to believe the group authentically wants what is in their best interests.

Some suggestions for engaging in healthy dialogue with your loved one to enhance both cultural humility and competence are: 1. Use reflective listening by authentically trying to grasp what they are telling you (e.g., "What I am hearing you say is…"), 2. Do not pass judgment on their lifestyle or beliefs, and 3. Express empathy (e.g., "I can truly feel the loneliness and sadness you are going through.").

One consistent cultural attribute shared by nearly all of the groups I have worked with in my clinical work or support groups is community, the degree of togetherness and strong bonds among members. Whether the cultural identification is based on ethnic, racial, or social aspects, there is a strong sense of community. With community, goals can be achieved and needs met on both individual and group levels when members selflessly work together. This cohesiveness among family members and desire to come together to support one another are all major factors, when present, which yield the best result for the families and loved ones.

Age considerations

Though the disease does not discriminate across ages, the skills discussed in this book are intended for family members of adult age. This consideration is important, because some of the strategies may result in extreme measures, such as not allowing an unwell family member to remain at home or withholding shelter or resources if they are unwilling to meet recovery expectations. As you can imagine, these strategies would not be appropriate for minors. While the "25 Must Knows" and many of the strategies are relevant to working with minors, some of the more extreme measures are appropriate for those of adult age. For those families who are in desperate need of interventions for minors, contact your pediatrician or your child or adolescent's therapist or school counselor for guidance.

Use of statistics and content validity

This book is not saturated with statistics and research studies; any data is drawn from emergent themes in my work with countless numbers of families and clients. Several thousand male and female adult clients have matriculated through the treatment program. Working with hundreds of families has provided me opportunities to analyze various family dynamics. My role at the adult residential treatment facility for clients struggling with substance addiction and/or mental health has allowed me to work directly with a predominant number of these clients and families at the individual, group, and family level. These clients and families come from all over the United States and are comprised of different races, cultures, ages, and socio-economic statuses. There is a range of religious beliefs, sexual orientations, and educational levels. Each family has a unique set of dynamics. Additionally, my private practice work has included clients struggling at all levels of acuity, with wide-ranging substance use and psychiatric conditions. Lastly, in my nearly ten years and counting working with families in crisis in my family support group, and through numerous talks I have presented in the community, I have assisted hundreds of families in desperate need of getting their loved ones help.

My wide experience working with an expansive number of individuals and families provides the basis for the data I drew from to write this guide. Furthermore, any statistics mentioned in the book, unless cited otherwise, are qualitative estimates and anecdotal evidence based on clients and families with whom I have intimately worked, and not data attained via quantitative measures and analyses. However, the only quantitative statistic used are frequency estimations. For instance, in Chapter 5, I will discuss the three most consistent factors I've noted differentiating individuals who progress in the treatment and recovery processes from those who do not. Along similar lines, I discuss in Chapter 9 the most re-occurring or frequent attributes often noted in family units able to break old, dysfunctional patterns of behaving and attain successful breakthroughs with their struggling loved ones.

The diversity of cases I have come across and the assortment of family populations I have assisted provide the ability to draw some general and consistent conclusions across individuals and families. Of course, as in most research, there are limits to the generalizability of the information due to the sample size and specific populations of focus (e.g., highly acute or in crisis).

Lastly, in order to substantiate the information, over fifteen subject matter experts (SMEs) and reviewers read the draft of this book and provided critical feedback. These SMEs were comprised of a combination of board-certified psychiatrists and psychologists, licensed therapists, social workers, certified addiction specialists and life coaches, as well as leaders in mental health and substance addiction organizations. The SMEs all varied in age, gender, race, years in practice, and theoretical orientations. The majority of SMEs had clinical experience working in both mental health and addiction capacities at outpatient and residential levels. In addition to non-professionals who work in mental health and/or addiction, I also asked individuals and families who have successfully navigated through the treatment process to review the book and offer their critiques.

Some of the core areas I asked these SMEs and experienced individuals and families to assess were: comprehensiveness of information (thoroughness and completeness of content), content validity (accuracy of information), information relevance (how pertinent the information is for the target audience), cultural considerations (does author address cultural diversity in the book), usefulness of skills taught (are tactics helpful for the target population), generalizability (information's ability to be used across diverse populations), readability (flow and ease of reading), applicability (appropriateness of information for the target population), and practicality (how feasible and practical is the information and skills taught in book). I thoughtfully considered all of their feedback and made the appropriate revisions to the final draft of the book.

Chapter 3

Understanding the Disease

This chapter will take a deeper look at the diseases of mental illness and substance abuse—the attributes, patterns, and manifestations. Though I share my conceptualization of the disease in bits and pieces throughout the book, this chapter will hopefully provide the foundational knowledge to further understand my perspective.

Remember, I personify the disease as a chronic entity that causes varying levels of impairment. By that definition, we all have our own version of disease. I also refer to the disease as an opponent or adversary to make it tangible, allowing us to recognize its vulnerabilities and devise a strategy to manage and beat it.

Attributes of the disease

In the substance abuse recovery arena, the untreated disease is described as *cunning (secretive and deceptive), baffling (complicated and complex),* and *powerful (highly influential),* as well as *unmanageable (chaotic and troublesome)* when not treated. It can render a person *powerless.* I wholeheartedly agree with each of those attributes. Sometimes people are reticent to accept the notion of powerlessness, under the presumption that they are relinquishing power over the disease or have become defenseless against it. I tell families *powerless* simply means you can't do it on your own. If you try to take on the disease one-on-one, you will most likely lose that battle. Fellowship and support systems are critical components keeping the disease at bay. The disease despises people who flock in healthy fellowship, as it loses its capacity to isolate the person; it wields the most powerful leverage when one-on-one. Anyone who has attained a level of success in any major arena of their life will never say they did it all on their own. Most likely, they had some help, encouragement, or influence somewhere along the way, whether it was a coach, mentor, teacher, peer, or family member.

When untreated, the disease is also *ageless*. Like a vampire, it can survive for a very long time, sucking the life out of you and anyone else it encounters. The way a vampire or disease survives is by multiplying (infecting) hosts (people). Once it doesn't have any more hosts to infect, its power is greatly diminished.

The disease is also *manipulative*, meaning it gets others to do things they normally would not do. There are thousands of ways to manipulate, such as using emotions, lying, blaming, playing victim, bullying, threatening verbally, utilizing guilt, playing naive, using money, knowledge, or sex, etc. At times, it may seem the disease is always four moves ahead, a perpetual checkmate you are powerless over.

The disease is also *progressive*, meaning it only gets worse when untreated. Barring a spiritual intervention or some tragic experience causing an immediate wake-up call (though, even in this case, it's not guaranteed), the likelihood of a person returning to a healthy baseline without help is not probable, especially when they have been struggling with their disease for a long time at moderate-to-severe levels.

I was fortunate to know and collaborate with a former trauma surgeon for the military who integrated military terminologies and war-related descriptions into his psychiatric work. One of the most salient descriptions he used to describe the disease was "the terrorist in the home." That description made a lot of sense to me. What does a terrorist do? It alters your lifestyle and makes you live in fear and walk on eggshells, worrying about its deceptive nature and willingness to attack at any moment. I tell families the terrorist disease will hold them emotionally hostage if they don't take action against it. Often family members can relate to feeling like a prisoner in their own home, with the disease running the household. One family member added, "The disease is taking up space in our home and not even paying us rent."

Another metaphor for the disease I like to use to educate family members is that of a traditional car (not talking about electric vehicles or battery-operated cars). In this case, guilt is the engine oil and fear the gas. The car can run somewhat efficiently for quite some time as long as it has these two critically important resources. The emotions of guilt and fear (along with all emotions) are not inherently bad, but they are your mind and body's response to some stimuli and can be "data points" to further explore. When emotions are overwhelming, severe, debilitating, or paralyzing, they become problematic. Guilt may serve as the impetus for change and fear can serve as a motivating factor or a survival mechanism to avoid danger. But feeding the disease guilt and fear will increase its ability to thrive and keep going.

Lastly, you should be aware of one more attribute of the disease. It's essential to understand that your loved ones share a very *intimate relationship* with their disease. They use a substance, engage in a dysfunctional pattern of behavior, or use manipulative tactics "because it works!" I will discuss this "because it works" concept more in Chapter 4, but keep in mind the intimate relationship means there is a connection your loved one has created with certain attributes of the disease that works for whatever they initially intended (e.g., drink alcohol to repress memories, lying to evade accountability, playing victim to attain support, etc.) Similarly, those who have been chronically struggling have developed a sense of comfort in their lifestyle, however emotionally painful, distressful, toxic, and chaotic it may be. Someone who has been struggling with debilitating depression for many years has likely become comfortable in the way of life accompanying it (e.g., isolation, negative thinking, self-loathing, lack of motivation and purpose). Clients have also shared how alcohol, their drug of choice, or unhealthy coping tools were the "only things that worked" to get them through traumas, deep-rooted pain, and unending hopelessness.

In some instances, unhealthy, maladaptive coping tools may have even saved their lives (e.g., using alcohol to drown out traumatic memories of abuse in order not to harm oneself, methamphetamines to conjure enough energy to be around others rather than isolate and think of ways to die, or marijuana to help sleep and not stay up all night in anger). Essentially, your loved one became dependent on the unhealthy life preserver buoying them through storms and have a legitimate fear of giving up the very thing saving them. Your loved ones have a close, intimate relationship with their dysfunctional life preserver, one they may grieve when it's gone. Clients in treatment have told me, "You mean I can never party again, or go drinking with my buddies?" or "I can never get high again?" I tell them they always have that option because, at the end of the day, no one can ever completely dictate their ability to decide what kind of life they want to live. However, that old option may no longer be conducive to a healthy life, or one their family members will be willing to support. I invite them to pursue the creation of a new, healthy life preserver and offer them a preview of what this other positive life may look and feel like through the treatment process. In other words, I offer them the opportunity to start a new journey—one with meaningful, life-altering outcomes.

Always remember the positive attributes of your loved ones

Amidst the dark talk of the disease, I think it's important to shed some hope and light. I continually remind family members to remember who their loved ones were before their struggles began. During group sessions, I instruct families to brag about their loved ones in treatment. I hear descriptive words such as smart, ambitious, loving, compassionate, artistic, athletic, giving, free-spirited, altruistic, spiritual, honest, and on and on. Likewise, clients often will abandon modesty to reveal things about themselves their peers didn't know. I am always floored by what I hear. My groups have included successful business owners, artists, entrepreneurs, scholars, teachers, healthcare professionals, award recipients, graduate school students, volunteers for the less fortunate, world travelers, aspiring professional athletes, high-level educators, parents, grandparents, etc. This exercise is invaluable for both family members and clients. It's so easy to forget these positive aspects and someone's potential, especially in treatment when the focus is on topics such as loss, regret, people they have hurt or lost, opportunities they have missed, people who have harmed them, and years they have "wasted." Remember, the disease does not define anyone! For some time, the disease may have infiltrated and taken over. With diligent effort, families and their loved ones can begin to understand its patterns and behaviors, learn to manage and defeat it, and begin to reconnect with one another in healthy ways.

The disease can always be a threat

It's important to accept the reality that the disease will always be present. If someone has been chronically struggling at a high enough level to cause significant impairment, the disease—even after long-term recovery—will always be a potential threat. To further accentuate this concept, there is a saying in the substance recovery arena that "the disease is always in the corner doing push-ups."

Figuratively speaking, if the disease was ninety percent of a person's being prior to treatment, a hopeful goal is that it will comprise approximately fifteen percent of their existence after treatment. It will never be zero percent, especially if they have chronically struggled with their conditions for many years. These conditions will always have the propensity to re-emerge under the right conditions (e.g., life altering events, high degrees of chronic stress, distancing from their recovery program, or engaging in old, dysfunctional patterns). When your loved ones minimize the disease's impact, they open wide the door to the positive aspects of their lives. But we should always respect the capabilities of our disease because, in a perfect storm, it will gain power again.

If we imagine a radar screen, the disease is at the center for your recovering family members prior to treatment and will move towards the outer edges after treatment and with strong recovery. Then, their responsibility becomes doing whatever it takes to avoid perfect storms (e.g., sustained chronic stress levels, consistent isolation, untreated depression, etc.) to keep the disease on the periphery of their radars. The disease will always be on your loved one's screen, but it's important to keep it in the outer areas—meaning, the disease no longer has a profound impact on their lives.

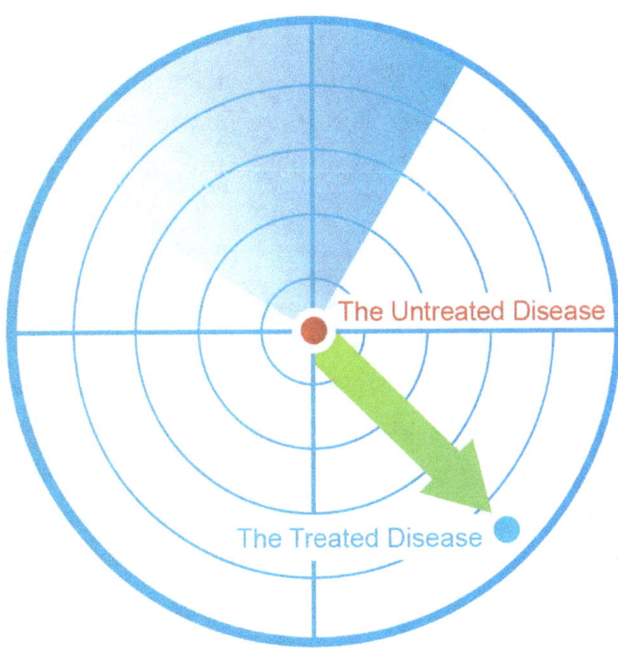

This concept is the same for someone with a history of alcoholism and drug addiction. After decades of sobriety, a person still needs to stay vigilant and respect the proficiency of the disease. The disease's sole purpose is to survive, and it's "game-on" when willing players step up. Like hypertension, diabetes, or other chronic conditions, under the perfect conditions (e.g., stress, poor diet, relentless triggers), addiction will flare up again and will always need to be managed.

Some of the disease's scariest words or phrases

Some of the most frightening words I hear a person say during their struggle in treatment or during long-term recovery are, "I got this," "I can manage my substance use," or "My mental health issues will no longer be a problem." A common action that puts clients at risk for relapse or lapse is taking themselves off their psychiatric medications without the collaboration of the prescribing medical provider. When people suddenly stop their psychiatric medications (e.g., anti-depressants, mood stabilizers, anti-anxiety meds, etc.), they may not feel the adverse symptoms at first (note: varying traces or residual concentrations of medications may still be in their systems) and assume they no longer need them. But there can be a rebound effect after a few days or weeks (note: when medications are no longer in their system or present in very small levels), when they'll experience a sudden flare of their symptoms (e.g., heightened sadness, anxiety, panic attacks, mania, etc.). It's also important to note the many dangers of suddenly stopping benzodiazepines (anti-anxiety medications), especially if they were being over-used. Seizures, panic attacks, palpitations, or sleep disturbances can occur. This rebound effect can be dangerous mentally and physically, which is why it's essential your recovering family members work out a treatment plan with their physician if they want to adjust the dosage or stop taking their medications.

After a period of sobriety, clients may believe they can manage their consumption (e.g., only have one glass of wine, a single bottle of beer, one hit of marijuana, etc.). I can honestly say, the odds of someone "managing" or "controlling" their substance use after a chronic struggle or a family history of substance addiction—especially with a co-occurring psychiatric condition—are heavily unfavorable. In fact, the likelihood of returning to that dark place once the door is opened is a safe bet. There's a saying in substance recovery: "Think of the last time you used (drugs) or drank. That is about as good as it gets." For most people in treatment, the last time they used substances was an extremely bad situation that certainly would worsen if they went back to their old habits. If I was asked to put a Vegas bet on it, I would wager one hundred percent *against* "safely managing" or "completely controlling" the substance use under these circumstances.

A powerful, personal account of the disease

One of the most powerful and provocative poems I have ever come across is titled, "I Am Your Disease," written by someone identified only as Joanne. In a detailed and vivid manner, she eloquently describes her disease, the intimate relationship they share, and her powerlessness over it. Remarkably, in the second half of the poem Joanne reveals her playbook on how to manage or defeat the disease (e.g., establishing strong fellowship, making better choices, surrendering to a healthy lifestyle, etc.).

<u>I Am Your Disease</u>

by Joanne

You know who I am, you've called me your friend
Wishes of misery and heartache I send
I want only to see that you're brought to your knees
I'm the devil inside you, I am your disease

I'll invade all your thoughts, I'll take hostage your soul
I'll become your new master, in total control
I'll maim your emotions, I'll run the whole game
Till your entire existence is crippled with shame

When you call me, I come, sometimes in disguise
Quite often I'll take you by total surprise
But take you I will, and just as you've feared
I'll want only to hurt you, with no mercy spared

If you have your own family, I'll see it destroyed
I'll steal every pleasure in life you've enjoyed
I'll not only hurt you, I'll kill if I please
I'm your worst living nightmare, I am your disease

I bring self-destruction, but still you can't tell

I'll sweep you through heaven, then drop you in hell
I'll chase you forever, wherever you go
And then when I catch you, you won't even know

I'll sometimes lay silent, just waiting to strike
What's yours becomes mine, cos I take what I like
I'll take all you own, and I won't care who sees
I'm your constant companion…I am your disease

If you have any honor, I'll strip it away
You'll lose all your hope and forget how to pray
I'll leave you in darkness, while blindly you stare
I'll reduce you to nothing, and won't even care

So, don't take me for granted, my powers are sublime
I'll bend, and I'll break you, time after time
I'll crumble your world with the greatest of ease
I'm that madman inside you…I am your disease

But today I'm real angry…you want to know why?
I let all in recovery, entirely slip by
How did I lose you? Where did I go wrong?
One minute I had you…then next you were gone

You just can't dismiss all the good times we've shared
When you were alone…wasn't it I who appeared?
When you sold those possessions you knew you would need
Wasn't I the first one who stepped in and agreed

Now look at you bastards, you're all thinking clear
You escaped with your lives when you found your way here
Only fools think they're winners when admitting defeat
It's what you must say when you're claiming that seat

Go ahead and surrender, if that's what you choose
But, I'm not giving up, cos I can't stand to lose
So stand in your groups and support hand in hand
Better choices will save you…leaving me to be damned

Well, be damned all you people seeking treatment each week
Be damned higher power, however unique
Be damned all your sayings, be damned your clichés
Be damned every addict, who back to me strays

For I know it will happen, I've seen it before
Those who love misery will crawl back for more
So take comfort in knowing, I'm waiting right here
But next time around, you'd just better beware

You think that you're stronger or smarter this time
There isn't a mountain or hill you can't climb
Well if that's what you're thinking, you ain't learned a thing
I'll still knock you silly if you step back in my ring

But you say you've surrendered, so what can I do?
It's so sad in a way, I had big plans for you
Creating your nightmare for me was a dream
I'm sure gonna miss you…we made quite a team

So please don't forget me, I won't forget you
I'll stand by your side watching all that you do
I'm ready and waiting, so call if you please
I won't let you forget me…I am your disease

When I read this poem to clients, they are often emotional, stating how realistic and similar it is to how they conceptualize their own disease. In fact, one female client became angry with me for reading it in a group therapy session, as it made her realize how intimately intertwined she'd become with alcohol and her depression, and how fearful she was about giving them up. Essentially, she wondered how she'd survive without these two entities, the familiar aspects of her life for the past decade. However, she, too, acknowledged the silver lining in the poem and realized she has power to no longer allow the disease to define her. By viewing her alcoholism and depression as separate entities from herself, she was able to come up with a plan to separate from them.

I hope I've been able to help you understand that the more we personify the disease as a separate entity, the better we'll be able to discover its manageable vulnerabilities. In Chapters 5 and 6, I will discuss specific strategies and ways to manage the disease.

Important Note:

The scariest words I ever hear someone say in recovery are "I got this" or "I can totally manage my (fill in drug of choice or mental health diagnosis)." The disease needs to be respected, always, due to the devastating power it can wield when taken for granted.

Chapter 4
25 Must Knows

This chapter includes what I believe is the most critical information every family needs to navigate the process of getting your struggling family members into treatment. I am a strong believer in knowledge as a first line of defense, and this chapter will provide the backbone and foundation for creating the strategic family plan.

Most families struggling for some time have already done their due diligence to become educated about the diagnosis/es of their loved one (if known) and are knowledgeable about any substances being used (if applicable) and some of the potential treatments and approaches. This information is only the beginning, however. My "25 Must Knows" serve as foundational knowledge for everyone involved in the family support system throughout the recovery process, but most essentially during the Pre-treatment Zone. These concepts may present as a mix of common and unique knowledge for some readers, but the discussion in these pages should provide a clearer understanding of the disease and the challenges it presents, no matter the person's degree of background knowledge and experience.

I have successfully coached hundreds of family members about how to get their loved ones into treatment. The spectrum of diagnoses and levels of acuity amongst the struggling individuals were wide-ranging in degree, and the families were struggling at varying levels as well. Some family members had recently learned of a loved one's diagnoses, while others had been attempting to help for years or decades. Additionally, my clients included clinicians and addiction specialists. After getting their loved one on a healthier path, most wished they'd known this important information earlier.

Must Know #1: Know to Have Hope, Know Treatment Works!

What the Disease May Tell You

> *For Liz, treatment is a waste of time and money, if it hasn't worked by now.*
> *Kim is too far gone in her addiction. You might as well give up.*
> *There is no coming back from psychosis.*
> *You have a strong family history of addiction, so the odds are bleak for Thomas.*

Why important:

Many family members and struggling loved ones lose hope and don't realize they still have power to make changes to their strategy.

One powerful, case example that demonstrates how a support team collaborating with a family filled with hope can make dramatic changes in the critical treatment process is a family whose grandson was having severe struggles with both substance abuse and mental illness. A user of methamphetamines, he'd been experiencing a manic episode (i.e., less need for sleep, goal-directed activities, grandiose delusions) for over two weeks and was psychotic (i.e., experiencing auditory hallucinations) from a lack of sleep. He was filled with resentment towards his grandparents and siblings for holding boundaries and putting him into treatment. He also had a strong desire to leave the facility. In our first session, he stated his plans to kill his grandparents and other family members with a gun, due to their decision to send him to treatment. I knew his thoughts and plans were due to his mania and psychosis but didn't know how much credence I should give them.

It is worth noting that I was obligated to report the threatening statements to law enforcement, because he identified victims and intentions and had the means to carry out the threat. Fortunately, the threat was greatly minimized by circumstance. His gun was in the care of a relative and, while in treatment, he was a few hundred miles away from his grandparents, with no car or money. Essentially, the threat was not imminent. The Sheriff knew the client was in early treatment and cognitively impaired but agreed it was appropriate to file a report regarding the statements, in the unlikely instance he followed through with his plan.

After two weeks, with abstinence from methamphetamines, regular medication, meals and sleep, the patient's entire mindset changed drastically. His family was involved in the treatment process all along, showing up for loving, emotional visits which renewed intimate connections and helped him feel supported. This case illustrates how impactful the treatment process can be. People can change—sometimes quickly—once they set forward on the path to healthier living.

When individuals are active participants in the treatment process, success often follows. Having a family support system in which each member understands their role is a big part of the journey to recovery. I will speak more about the critical factors that allow clients to flourish in recovery and the attributes family members should possess to aid the process. For now, maintain hope. It is one of the most critical assets, from treatment through recovery.

The Take Home:

Trust in the treatment process. As long as there is hope, there is a chance.

Must Know #2: Know That It Takes More Than Just Willpower

What the Disease May Tell You

> *If Lorraine really wanted to stop drinking, she could.*
> *Barry can get out of his depression if he thinks positively.*
> *Gladys isn't really delusional. She can rationalize herself out of those crazy beliefs.*

Why important:

Sometimes, family members and struggling loved ones falsely believe that powering through with willpower is all one needs to do. They fail to realize that a multifactorial strategy (having many elements and facets) will maximize long-term success.

A common misconception I hear from family members relates to the role of willpower in the treatment process. According to BetterHelp (betterhelp.com), *willpower* is "a type of strength that assists with controlling thoughts and behaviors" and *will* is "the ability to choose one's own actions;" hence, willpower is a strong ability for self-determination. Families cling to the belief that struggling loved ones can simply will or force themselves ("white knuckle") past their adversities. The most effective approach in my work with families has been a comprehensive one (e.g., treatment, therapy, support groups, etc.) that factors in willpower but addresses the complexities associated with the loved ones' struggles.

People who have chronically struggled often reach a point of physical, mental, and social impairment. When clients present to treatment or attend private sessions with me, it's likely their struggles have been issues for a long period of time. They no longer need help for one event or experience; these struggles have overflowed into many other areas of their lives. Certainly, isolated events such as a car accident, sexual assault, or another heightened stressor can be an initial cause for struggle, but more likely, other contributing factors have gone untreated for an extended period of time, exacerbating their overall struggles, which is why comprehensive support is more critical than sole willpower. For instance, when someone experiences a stroke, that medical event is a direct cause for challenges. However, if the recovery process takes several years, other issues may arise. The person may deal with depression from social isolation or lose motivation because of the slow progress in rehabilitation. They may start drinking alcohol or using substances to cope with feelings such as resentment or helplessness. Any of these could be collateral effects from the initial event of the stroke.

> **The Take Home:**
>
> Know that willpower is only one factor in the healing process. The best outcome will occur with a comprehensive treatment approach.

Must Know #3: Know to Have Hope in Neuroplasticity

What the Disease May Tell You

It's too late. Sunny has been doing meth for years, and his brain will never mend.

Uncle Brad has been depressed for decades. He will never have a positive outlook on life.
Sally has suffered so much trauma in her life, and there is no way she will love herself again.

Why important:

After losing hope that their loved ones may ever change or get healthy again, many family members give up on the possibility of positive change due to the chronic mental damage their loved ones endured. Essentially, family members may believe it's too late to get back to a healthy normal.

Neuroplasticity is the theory that postulates the human brain's capacity to heal, adapt, change, grow, and create new memories throughout a person's lifetime. This ability to "re-wire" or repair itself and create neuronal connections is a promising concept, especially for those struggling with psychiatric conditions, physical or emotional traumas, or addictions over a long period of time. Our brains are resilient and adaptable. For many family members concerned their loved ones may never be able to recover and fully function after dealing with severe substance abuse or untreated mental health issues, neuroplasticity provides good news.

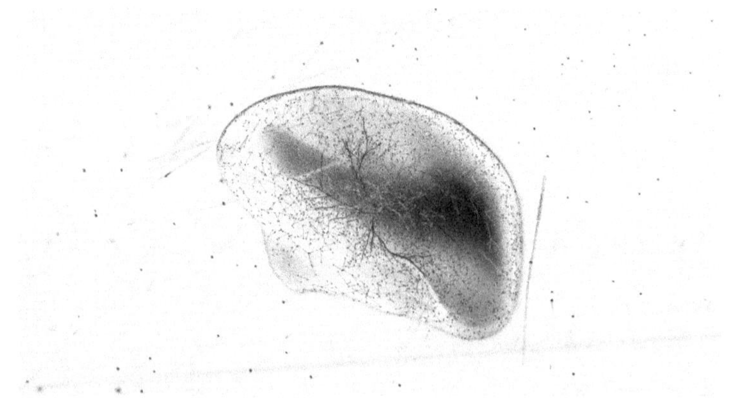

As with any promising concept, however, there are limits to note. Though neuroplasticity speaks to the human body's resilience and profound capacity to grow and heal, it doesn't imply an infinite threshold to what our brains can endure. In other words, at some point a person can do so much damage that coming back may be less probable, which is why it's imperative to get loved ones help sooner rather than later.

Neuroplasticity also suggests that the human brain tends to gravitate towards familiarity as opposed to novelty (the quality of being new). Familiarity requires less adaptation compared to novelty, which can involve discomfort and stress. For instance, people who have struggled for long periods of time with substance abuse or mental illness may have reached a level of comfort in their unhealthy way of life, due to familiarity. Frequently, I have discussions with chronically depressed clients who confirm a sense of comfortableness in their depression. They say, "It's all I know." Getting better is new and foreign ground. Equally importantly, I have heard families state they find themselves acquiescing to their loved one's way of life by associating the person with the disease, allowing them to stay stuck in their illness (e.g., not holding them accountable, not motivating them or assigning responsibilities, etc.). This comfort in adopting a certain way of life can be the same for someone diagnosed with schizophrenia, bipolar disorder, anxiety disorders, learning disabilities, or substance use disorder. Some dangerous statements I have heard from family members with chronically struggling loved ones are, "That's just Sarah being Sarah," "We've tried helping Roger, but he's too old to change," "Yes, I know we walk on eggshells around Mackenzie and her angry outbursts, but it's better than provoking her."

When a family gets comfortable with an unhealthy lifestyle, that narrative can start to solidify, causing a "new normal" or "new baseline" to result for the person struggling. And, because neuroplasticity shows that our minds move towards familiarity, this familiar lifestyle can create a hard-fast narrative that will be harder to change the longer it remains. The longer a person remains in a heightened, acute state, the closer they get to reaching a point of little-to-no return.

In a continuing education seminar titled "Reasoning with Unreasonable People: Focus on Disorders of Emotional Regulation," I learned a technique suggested for use in the first session interview, when trying to disrupt narratives. The psychologist leading the session, Joseph Shannon, PhD, described the following tactic. When he meets with a new client (presumably not someone highly acute, in acute trauma, suicidal, or psychotic), he tells them, "You have 7.5 minutes to tell me your life story." Dr. Shannon didn't state why he chose 7.5 minutes, but I assume he felt that was long enough for a person to provide a general overview of their struggles. Once the time elapses, he then tells the client, "Now, you can no longer tell me that story in the same way again without revising it." He wasn't implying that the client's story was invalid or inconsequential. He was trying to illustrate that he'd be doing them more harm than good if he allowed them to tell the same story each week, without making necessary changes or modifications.

Please note: specific treatment methods exist for working on neuroplasticity. Changing a person's narrative and way of life can be addressed with other modalities such as trauma-focused therapy, cognitive behavioral treatment, dialectical behavior therapy, narrative therapy, etc. Consult with a therapist or mental health professional for guidance on these treatment approaches.

The Take Home:

Have hope that your loved ones are more resilient than you may think. They have the ability to heal and get better, no matter what they have endured physically, emotionally or mentally.

Must Know #4: Know to Grant Permission to Release Yourself from Guilt

What the Disease May Tell You

You are the reason Fred is like this. You should have stopped his marijuana use a long time ago.

Divorcing when Nathan was five years old was a wrong decision.

Working two jobs and not being present is the reason Rajan is depressed.

You shouldn't have remarried so soon and introduced a stepparent.

Why didn't you listen to Jackie more?

You are an enabler.

You should have believed Candace when she first told you her boyfriend was abusing her.

> **Why important:**
>
> Guilt is one of the most debilitating emotions and one of the strongest impediments to family members getting their struggling family members help.

According to Merriam-Webster Dictionary, *guilt* is "a feeling of deserving blame for some action or lack thereof." It is a valid emotion and part of the human condition. However, in a chronic state, guilt can be paralyzing and prevent healthy action from taking place (e.g., boundary setting). I will speak on this issue later in the book, but know the disease thrives and, in many ways, survives on guilt. I firmly believe the only possible, positive aspect of guilt is its potential to be an impetus for change. I have seen hundreds of varying family dynamics in treatment, and guilt is one of the most common, crippling emotions. Guilt serves as an impediment and a major reason why family members do not pull the proverbial trigger and take the necessary steps to get their loved ones help. Guilt will hold the family emotionally hostage in its solid grip, limiting their ability to make the critical moves needed.

A case example is that of a young, female adult, an only child whose parents smoked marijuana recreationally. One day, this fourteen-year-old asked about marijuana, and both parents decided to teach her the responsible way to smoke it. They preferred she learned from them rather than being taught irresponsible methods. When the family came to see me, the girl had become addicted to marijuana, opiates, and alcohol. The father suffered immense guilt, believing he was the sole reason she had become an addict. Because of this guilt, it took five years before he and his wife finally realized they couldn't shoulder all the responsibility of helping her. I simply asked him, "Did you intentionally mean to harm your daughter? Did you aim for her to be an addict?" His response was a quick, "Absolutely not." I told him, "Let go of guilt. This disease thrives on it." Eventually, their daughter completed treatment and started the path to long-term sobriety.

In the treatment process, I have encountered thousands of family members dealing with problematic family dynamics. I would estimate that ninety-nine percent of these people acted in good faith, without intentional harm, like the parents above. Sometimes family members make counterproductive decisions or fail to choose the best options, but they almost always do not mean true harm. The one percent who do are usually substance abusers themselves, suffering from a severe, untreated mental illness, and/or are in a psychotic state.

One way to ease the burden of self-directed guilt is to take action contrary to the problematic behaviors a person engages in. This is also known as "amends" in substance recovery. It simply means taking ownership and attempting reconciliation for past wrongdoings. According to *Oxford English Dictionary, amends* means "to correct." Some examples of ways to make amends include becoming a more active listener (if you minimized one's cries for help), being better informed (if you avoided topics you were not comfortable with), presenting as a healthy role model (if you struggled with self-responsibility), or heightening awareness (if you were insensitive to another's cultural needs)—all of these amends should focus on the actions that made you feel guilty in the first place. Moreover, if there is emotional guilt surrounding the idea that these amends should have taken place a long time ago, I tell my clients (who struggle with guilt for not getting healthier/ sober sooner) or family members (who feel they should have acted more quickly), that the two best times to have made these changes were back **THEN** (when they thought the change should have taken place) and **NOW**. This powerful statement helps people get unstuck and resolve guilt about not making positive changes sooner. Please, do not give guilt any more power than it already has. The disease uses it as fuel to extend its stay.

The Take Home:

Press the reset button, and don't allow lingering guilt to fuel the disease.

Must Know #5: Know That Enabling is Not a Curse Word

What the Disease May Tell You

You are a bad person for loving Shelly too much.

Your overly big heart got Roy to this crisis point.

Giving Priti money all the time is why she's an addict.

Getting Xioa that apartment and money for college provided the opportunity for him to use drugs, isolate, and harm himself.

Why important:

Sometimes family members engage in behaviors they believe are helpful and nurturing, but, in fact, perpetuate the problems.

Many family members who come to me hold fast to the notion that enabling is an inherently bad word, and something to avoid on all levels. In support groups, enabling is such an unfavorable word that some end up harboring a great level of shame for showing compassion to their unwell loved ones.

When addressing substance abuse in the support group arena, families are introduced to the *3 C's*. They are told, "You didn't Cause It, Can't Control It, and Can't Cure It." I will often add, "But you have contributed or perpetuated it in some form or fashion, sometimes through enabling." Even if they know enabling wasn't helpful and might put their loved ones in harm's way, family members rarely mean intentional harm.

What a lot of people don't acknowledge is that enabling comes from a place of care, love, and nurturance. It's what we do as parents or family members. Also, just because a person (or family) is acting out of love, it might not be the best or most productive method. Sometimes, it can actually be dysfunctional and counterproductive when trying to help someone. When our significant ones are hungry, we give them nourishment; when they are homeless, we provide them shelter; when they are jobless, we offer resources. When a person is perpetually struggling with unhealthiness, enabling becomes problematic if it diminishes the person's motivation to take contrary action and get help. Withholding some of these things doesn't mean you stop caring for your loved one, it just means the love needs to come in a different form. I call this type of caring *assertive love*, and I will talk about it next in *Must Know #6*.

The Take Home:

Keep caring for your struggling family members and realize your love needs to be expressed differently when battling the disease.

Must Know #6: Know to Use Assertive Love Over Tough Love

What the Disease May Tell You

Shut Arya off completely. She obviously doesn't love you or want your help.

Let him go, even if that means he will die. That is probably what Axel wants and might be the best scenario for the family.

Evander obviously doesn't need you, so why waste your time and energy trying to help him?

> **Why important:**
>
> Family members sometimes believe being tough requires withholding the expression of love, but this approach ends up creating more disconnect from the struggling loved one.

Tough love has its appropriate place and is usually well-meaning in intention. The challenge is making sure tough love isn't interpreted as a cessation of love and care. What people may inadvertently hear when someone says, "tough love" is "tough luck." Family members who have participated in support groups tell me they interpret "tough love" as completely shutting the person out of their lives—essentially, stonewalling them (an extreme level of avoidance or refusal to cooperate or communicate with someone, e.g., silent treatment, at all costs). This approach may communicate to the unwell family member that no support or options remain, which can cause hopelessness, a major risk factor for suicidality. When a lack of hope is present, giving up altogether is the likely result. Throughout the process of getting help for your loved one, you may need to activate some behaviors that portray toughness, without eliminating the love and care component. You can still plant the seeds of care, reassuring your loved ones you will always love them, while expressing that you are no longer able to support their current, unhealthy lifestyle.

I prefer to use the term "assertive love" with families as one of the essential, boundary-setting skills in getting their loved ones help. There is a classic saying I once noticed in an elementary classroom and have never forgotten: "Rules without relationships breed rebellion; relationship without rules breeds contempt." My interpretation of this is when a person is too bound by rules (i.e., too many directives, mandates, orders, rules) and does not have a connection or bond (i.e., too little relationship) with another, that person will rebel against them. Contrarily, if a person is buddy-buddy (i.e., too much relationship) with diffuse boundaries (i.e., very little rules), when a boundary or rule is implemented, they will resist out of a sense of entitlement or superiority. I have found in both my clinical work and personal experience that in every aspect of life where relationships are involved, the balance between relationship and rules tends to dictate the effectiveness of the relationship. This approach can include between spouses, parent to child, peer to peer, manager to employee, or among co-workers.

I will discuss *how* assertive love is integrated into the strategic plan in my *Must Know #13*. And in *Must Know #25*, I will talk more about a powerful tool in building relationships and a major component in assertive love—validation.

The Take Home:

Tough love does not mean tough luck.

It's imperative to continue loving and caring for your loved ones who are struggling to maintain hope. But love and care need to look different, with a balance between relationship (connection or bond) and rules (boundaries and limits).

Must Know #7: Know That Everyone Needs to Pick Up an Oar (Assume Equal Responsibility)

What the Disease May Tell You

Ava has been using substances for years. She needs to do all the work.

You did nothing wrong, so you don't have any changing to do.

All you did was love Archie, so why should you disrupt your life to get him help?

Why important:

At times, family members tend to think that the person who has caused the most emotional, mental, and physical hurt in the family (e.g., the person struggling with mental health or substance use) is the person who needs to do most of the work when, in fact, everyone in the primary support system needs to share in the responsibility for true change to happen. Thus the saying: "If nothing changes, nothing changes."

To best illustrate this *Must Know*, I use the analogy of a rowboat. If you've ever been on a paddle-powered vessel with others, you know the best way to maximize distance and speed is if everyone on the boat is assuming equal responsibility and doing their part. This doesn't imply that everyone on the boat needs to be equally skilled, strong, or knowledgeable about rowing. Everyone should share equal accountability, utilize individual strengths, and try their best.

In this analogy, the people on the boat are the most intimate members of the family circle (which I call the primary support system). They have the most influence on the struggling family member and are closely involved in trying to give support. There may be other important members in the fleet, but my book predominantly focuses on the people in the rowboat. If a family has five members (including the struggling loved one), everyone needs to assume twenty percent responsibility (100% divided by five individuals) and work one hundred percent on their individual share if they want full, comprehensive change for the family. A powerful question each member can ask to ensure shared accountability takes place is, "What can I change?" This inward focus prevents outward blaming and keeps the focus on aspects they have control over.

This concept is important because families tend to equate the degree to how much distress or harm (e.g., legal, financial, family problems, etc.) one has caused to the level of work that person needs to do. This notion also further assumes that those struggling less in the family have a smaller share of responsibility. For example, if a son has been in and out of recovery for years, his family may have the notion that he will have to do most of the work (maybe ninety percent). In these cases, the loved one feels alone and defeated, and believes everyone else does not need to make any revisions. This greatly reduces the chances for long-lasting change as the struggling person can feel overwhelmed and experience emotional abandonment in the process. Furthermore, some of the most problematic statements cited from a family member or multiple members when they consistently struggle with conflict resolution are "I did nothing wrong," and "It's not my fault." This blaming and lack of self-accountability problematically serve as major obstacles for effective communication and for reaching solutions. In order to accept a share of accountability, I suggest each family member in the primary support system ask, "What can I change for the betterment of myself and the family?"

Remember, family members need to accept they didn't "Cause it, can't Control it, and can't Cure it." But often, they enabled the disease, somehow. This perpetuation could have occurred in many ways. Let's use for an example a family of four, which includes a grandmother, father, mother, and son who all need to work one hundred percent on their personal share for the best, comprehensive outcomes. If the father grew up in a culture that minimized mental health, that lack of awareness is the twenty-five percent he needs to work on. If the mother struggles with a history of abuse that interferes with her ability to relate to her struggling son, that is her twenty-five percent. If the grandmother tends to enable her grandson by giving him money, that is the twenty-five percent she needs to work on. Lastly, if the son struggles with his bipolar disorder and alcohol use, that is his twenty-five percent. For each example, the individual's issues cause problems in the family unit that need to be addressed individually.

The Take Home:

Identify your share of accountability that may be perpetuating problems in your family unit. Then, pick up an oar and give one hundred percent effort as you share responsibility.

Must Know #8: Know Why They Do It: Because It Works! (Their Life Preserver)

What the Disease May Tell You

Kamal is abusing drugs for the plain fun of it, so he can stop whenever it's not fun anymore.

Jabari lies to you for no apparent reason.

Sophia threatening to kill herself is all about manipulation.

Marcia isolates herself from others because she is a hermit and hates people.

> **Why important:**
>
> Family members need to understand their loved ones are fearful of getting help when it means they will be asked to give up the very thing(s) they believe are keeping them functioning or alive.

One question I repeatedly ask families who have a member chronically struggling with substances or some maladaptive behavior(s) is, "Can you tell me in three words why your loved ones smoke marijuana incessantly, drink to oblivion, act out with rage, blame others for their issues, etc.?" Each time, everyone looks around the room with blank stares, hoping for prompts from others. When they do offer answers, they say things like, "To numb pain," "To get away," or, "To help forget." But all of those valid answers point to a broader one: "Because it works!"

First, substances. From smoking marijuana to help feel more relaxed in work meetings, to having a shot of vodka before a social event to take the edge off, to smoking cigarettes to lessen anxiety, to snorting cocaine to study for final exams, to taking benzodiazepines to forget about a traumatic event, people engage in substances because they work. Now, behaviors. When a loved one is using anger to get what they want, acting naïve to avoid responsibilities, isolating to ignore problems, or utilizing money to manipulate someone's decisions—all are examples of maladaptive behaviors people engage in "because they work."

I tell family members and struggling individuals they wouldn't be doing what they're doing if it didn't work. These unhealthy coping tools are what your untreated family members believe will bring balance, homeostasis, and equilibrium. Initially, these behaviors and substances work remarkably well in the way they were originally intended, but in time, the user develops a tolerance and the tools become ineffective, unhealthy, dysfunctional and counterproductive.

The support system needs to realize the substance (e.g., alcohol, marijuana, heroin, etc.) or maladaptive behavior (e.g., lying, isolation, playing victim, using guilt, etc.) serves as their family member's life preserver (a dysfunctional one), which kept them afloat temporarily but eventually will cause them to sink. Most people I see are fearful of treatment; many leave within the first week to thirty days. When those malfunctioning life preservers are taken away, they are required to stay afloat and survive alone. This triggers a great deal of distress. Treatment helps them create a healthier, productive, and resilient life preserver (e.g., healthy coping tools, better decision-making, positive attitude, etc.).

I discussed the "Because It Works!" notion as it applies to substances and behaviors. Another, more light-hearted way to illustrate the concept is an example we can all identify with—a young child wanting candy at the store. We've all been there, whether it was with our own kids or nieces and nephews, or we've witnessed another parent and child. At the checkout line, your young child asks for their favorite sweet. You say no, but the child cries and gives a gut-wrenching, sad face, and you relent, not only because of their irresistible, heartbreaking eyes, but also due to the line behind you and the stares from the checker. You tell yourself that next time, you will not give in. You'll hold your ground. During that next trip to the store, you stand firm, and your little one starts to cry after his request is denied. You hold your ground. Your precious one screams and thrashes on the floor. Again, out of sheer embarrassment for holding up the line and also because you notice the checker's impatient look, you angrily buy the candy bar.

When I present that scenario to families, I ask them what happened. If the young child doesn't get what he wants, he knows to turn up the level of his tantrum and you will have an emotional breaking point, eventually giving in. Thus, the unhealthy behavior is reinforced. The little child can throw a fit and get what he wants "because it works!" All he needed to do was turn up the intensity. This is what unwell people will do in the height of their struggles. They will push the limits and test your threshold by increasing the volume on the maladaptive behavior (e.g., threatening to harm themselves, stonewalling family members, or threatening to harm others) until you give in.

Chapter 7 will introduce some skills and statements you can use to set firm boundaries to avoid reinforcing negative, maladaptive behaviors.

> **The Take Home:**
>
> Help your loved ones abandon their maladaptive coping mechanisms (i.e., malfunctioning life preserver) by no longer allowing these tools to be used.

Must Know #9: Know Why They Keep Doing It and Refuse to Get Help—Because They Can!

What the Disease May Tell You

Let Tamika yell at you. She'll wake up one day and know she's wrong.
Jason is going through an angry stage and will snap out of it soon.
Don't enforce taking meds. Logan will get tired of hearing voices and will take them eventually.
Gabriel won't continue blaming you for his problems forever. He will grow up and take ownership."

> **Why important:**
>
> Many times, family members don't realize their well-intentioned actions are contributing to their untreated family members' chronic patterns and keeping them out of situations that would help them realize how maladaptive their behaviors are.

Once again, a common question I pose to families who have members continually engaging in unhealthy behavioral patterns is, "Do you know why your loved one keeps (abusing alcohol, losing jobs, going in and out of jail, using anger against you, getting away with lying, etc.)?" Again, baffled looks spread throughout the room as everyone looks around for answers. "Because they can!"

A classic example was a family who came to me for help with their grandson, a young man who abused methamphetamines and alcohol until he suffered fits of rage and substance-induced psychosis. During these outbursts, he would enter his grandparent's room in the early hours of the morning, knock down their bedroom door, yell obscenities, and blame them for his "miserable life." The grandfather had reinforced the door with bolts, but that hadn't stopped the grandson. I asked, "How many doors has he kicked down?" They responded, "Over ten." I asked, "Do you know why your grandson can knock down over ten doors?" They looked at each other blankly but could not come up with an answer. "Because he can!" In his unhealthy state, their grandson may have believed they were to blame. By not setting a firm boundary and allowing him to knock down so many doors, the grandparents may have been inadvertently reinforcing his belief that they were to blame, and his behaviors were not that bad. Once they held boundaries and put him in a situation forcing treatment, his blaming behaviors ceased.

Another case that comes to mind was a young adult who came to me after multiple, short-term stints in prior treatment. The longest time he'd ever clocked in treatment was three days. This time around, his father had remained adamant that he needed to complete treatment and would not be allowed to come home, no matter what. Three days in, the client registered every complaint in the book—the food wasn't being cooked properly, he wasn't getting along with peers, the staff weren't addressing his needs. This is the disease's way of building a case to leave. In the middle of a group session, this young man asked the staff if he could call his father. The client and father could be heard having a contentious conversation, and the father seemed to repeatedly state he must stay in treatment. The client said he would walk out if he needed to. Thirty minutes later, the father showed up and the son was waiting with his bags packed. The cycle was set on repeat, started all over again. Because it works and because he can!

The Take Home:

Break your loved ones' maladaptive patterns by eliminating enabling and by no longer co-signing their unhealthy lifestyle.

Must Know #10: Know to Accept the Inevitable Consequences of Untreated Mental Illness and Substance Abuse

What the Disease May Tell You

Hans can't die from alcohol abuse because he's only thirty-five years old.

It's much safer to allow Ginger to stay in the relationship with her husband, even if he is a cocaine addict. He works and provides for her and if they broke up, she might take her own life.

Imran is just manipulating you with his talk of dying. He won't really do it."

> **Why important:**
>
> Family members need to accept the potential consequences of their untreated family member not getting help. The insight needed to devise an action plan is delayed when they harbor immense fear and are paralyzed by worst-case outcomes.

Early in my clinical work, I learned an important concept from someone who had successfully achieved nearly four decades of sobriety from alcohol. In his support meetings, he learned there were three, inevitable consequences of untreated addiction: 1) jail, 2) institutions/hospitals, or 3) death. I believe these are the same potential consequences for people who chronically struggle with a moderate-to-severe psychiatric condition and never receive help. A fourth potential consequence I would add is homelessness, but eventually the homeless, without help, will end up in jail, institutions, or hospitals, or they will die.

The fear of losing a loved one to death is a potential outcome that precludes families from taking the necessary actions to get that unwell family member help. As a parent myself, one of my most unfathomable fears is outliving my children. This same fear I harbor is echoed by every single family I have ever worked with, and I'm sure any parent reading this would concur. Families may never be able to accept emotionally that a child or family member may die, but it is critically important to try to accept the possibility if they want to stop the loved one from spiraling down a dark path.

Here are a few cases that highlight how fear plays a role in preventing families from taking necessary action. First, a father and mother were aware their daughter, who lived upstairs, was abusing pain killers and alcohol, but that scenario seemed better than her being on the streets, where she could be sex trafficked or raped. Another example was a mother who knew her son, who lived in an apartment she paid for, was not using the money for college but to buy methamphetamines and cocaine. Lastly, a set of grandparents knew their granddaughter, who lived in their guesthouse, smoked marijuana, drank vodka, and suffered from hearing voices, but as long as she wasn't in jail or a hospital, they believed they were keeping her safe.

In each of these real-life scenarios, the families were trying to act from a good and caring place, but they were enabling. They believed they were preventing worst-case outcomes but didn't understand they were perpetuating the inevitable, worse outcome—jail, institutions, or death. The longer a loved one remains in an unhealthy state, the more likely these scenarios grow, due to the progressive nature of the disease. The chances of the person magically snapping out of it or getting better on their own are very slim. Furthermore, the longer they live in this severe degree of unhealthiness, the more comfortable they may become with this lifestyle, and the harder it is to get on the path to recovery. More intensive intervention and treatment will be required to have a successful recovery.

> **The Take Home:**
>
> Although it's painful to imagine, you must accept the reality that your loved ones may die if they don't get help.

Death and Suicidality

It's imperative to discuss the very important topics of death and suicide, as they tend to be the biggest fears preventing family members from taking the necessary actions to get help for their loved ones.

There are many misconceptions and myths about suicidality, which can be defined as thoughts, desires, intentions, or plans related to harming or killing oneself. Family members perpetuate many myths on this topic. Before we move on, I must stress that suicidality should always be taken seriously, even if you are uncertain about the likelihood of its occurrence, or the severity of a person's struggle. It's important to note that a person is seven times more likely to be successful with each subsequent suicide attempt. Therefore, any level of suicidality should not to be taken lightly. If you suspect your loved one is in danger of self-harm and needs help, contact the **National Suicide Prevention Lifeline:** Dial 988, or go to the 988 Suicide & Crisis Lifeline (988lifeline.org) or Speaking of Suicide (speakingofsuicide.com).

Myth 1: *If someone thinks about*
dying, they must want to die.

Not everyone who thinks about dying necessarily wants to end their life. Clients have told me they fantasize about not waking up one morning, or they've felt it wouldn't be so bad if they died in a car accident or didn't survive a stroke or heart attack. However, many of these people don't really want to die; they merely want their pain to stop. Family, religion, fear, and even pets—all can be reasons why someone would not act on their suicidal thoughts. A married client with no kids told me her three cats were the only things keeping her alive. I validated her by saying, "Your cats mean a lot to you. Now let's work on even more reasons to keep living." But the more a person entertains these thoughts, the more risk there is for them to gravitate towards a window of vulnerability. Those desires may turn into intentions, so it's important to get help.

Similarly, along with thoughts about self-harm, some behaviors are not imminently threatening but can steer a person toward more serious attempts. These actions are called parasuicidal behaviors. The *DSM-5* refers to these actions as *non-suicidal self-injury* (e.g., cutting on one's body parts with a razor, burning skin with a lighter, punching or hitting own body, speeding carelessly through traffic, reckless drug use such as sharing dirty needles, or intentionally consuming much more substances than usual, etc.). According to Comtois (2002), *parasuicidal behaviors* are any nonfatal, self-injurious behavior with a clear intent to cause bodily harm (but not necessarily with the intention of death).

Some family members believe their loved ones want to die when they engage in parasuicidal behaviors, but not realizing it may be a sign of distress and a call for help in saving them from venturing down the path of suicide. For instance, one family member stated, "Our daughter constantly cuts on her arms with a pin, so she must want to end her life." This behavior is concerning and should not be minimized but should also not immediately be considered imminent crisis level without further exploration. In many ways, these behaviors such as cutting or burning have become a form of coping skills for people, albeit an unhealthy one. Several clients have expressed that cutting themselves provided a sense of relief, made their emotions feel real, or offered a sense of self-control. Although these actions do not necessarily pose an imminent threat, the more a person engages in these behaviors, the likelihood of attempting suicide increases and becomes a real threat.

Tragically, many accidental deaths have occurred as a result of parasuicidal behaviors (e.g., substance overdoses, head trauma after repeatedly banging or hitting their own head, or a serious medical event after deep cutting behaviors). Therefore, it is very important to monitor parasuicidal behaviors and recognize the implications to a person's overall well-being—while also keeping in mind these behaviors don't unquestionably signify that a person wants to die. Vigilance and active monitoring are keys to safely gauging severity.

Myth 2: If they really wanted to die, they would have done it by now.

There are times when people talk about wanting to die and have sincere intentions and plans to do so. But they may be hesitant or scared or still have doubts. When someone talks about wanting to die but hasn't attempted suicide, the dangers of this thought process should still be taken seriously. As I mentioned earlier, it is critically important to seek some type of counseling or support. Also, there are times people may not present with obvious suicidality (e.g., still working at job, hanging out with friends and families, caring for kids), but deep down they have suicidal thoughts or intentions. Do not always assume that a person will accurately meet the textbook criteria of suicidality, or overtly present as suicidal to warrant attention. Outward appearances can belie internal struggle. It's important to be vigilant, to continue asking how they're doing, especially if they've had a history of suicidality or if you're concerned about underlying struggles they may be hiding.

Myth 3: *Suicide is a completely selfish act.*

Due to the deep emotional pain and void suicide can leave, a family may feel angry in its aftermath and come to this point of view that suicide is a completely selfish act. However, people contemplate suicide from such a dark place emotionally, with severely impaired thinking, and may believe ending their life is the "best selfless choice," "doing everyone a favor," "the only option they have left," or "relieving their family of the burden." In my experience, people in this state of crisis do not view themselves as being selfish, but rather, selfless along these lines of thinking. Again, it's important to get help at the first sign of suicidal thoughts.

Those who attempt suicide harbor a great deal of hopelessness, which further rationalizes the reasons they believe ending their lives is the best option. Statements like, "There is no hope," "What's the purpose?" "Why does living matter anymore?" reflect their convoluted thinking. Whenever someone is navigating through an immense amount of hopelessness, it can feel like cowering in the back of a dark, cold cave. The way out cannot be seen or is too distant; at this point, hope seems intangible and unachievable. Family members need to do whatever they can, in a healthy manner, to instill hope in their untreated family members. Let them know they are loved and will be supported if and when they decide to get help.

My *Must Know #19: Know to Keep Planting the Emotional Seeds*, will discuss ways to instill hopefulness in your loved ones, even if they continue to resist treatment.

Myth 4: Threats of suicide are pure manipulation.

There are cases when a person may make statements such as, "If you break up with me, what's the point of living?" "If I can't live here, I might as well not exist anymore," or "You don't want to support me. Why should I be alive any longer?" These statements may sound like manipulation or, in some scenarios, could be intended as such. Even when families are frustrated and scared and suspect manipulation, it's important to take threats seriously and monitor closely, as this way of self-destructive thinking is not normal or healthy. The person can greatly benefit from help to deal with these thoughts and learn other ways to cope with distress and communicate their needs more effectively.

In cases when someone may be using suicidal threats as a form of manipulation, a cry for help, or to make a serious threat, I counsel family members to respond, *"You sound very (insert emotion). You matter to me, and I want to help you. I wonder if you may need a higher level of care, or a professional to assist. Can we contact someone who can best help you? What can I do to help and support you?"* These validating statements will let your loved ones know they are being taken seriously, and that you will help provide assistance no matter what level of suicidality they are navigating through.

Myth 5: *Most people who attempt suicide truly want to die.*

Just as contemplating suicide doesn't necessarily reflect a will to die, most people who attempt suicide or contemplate suicide do not desire death but rather, an end to the emotional and/or physical pain. This has been the case with the majority of clients struggling with suicidality I've treated, including those who made an attempt. Although they feel hopeless and believe they have no other options, many actually want to live and have been searching for reasons to live. Certainly, some people truly do not want to live, but I believe these are outliers, rare cases; the majority are looking for an alternative to taking their own lives.

Myth 6: *People never have a change of mind once they make an attempt.*

I have worked with clients who changed their minds at the last moment of a suicide attempt. I have read interviews with people who experienced this change of mind after ingesting pills, trying to hang themselves, crashing a vehicle, using a gun on themselves, or leaping off a bridge. These survivors lived to tell of their ordeal; it's disheartening to think of those who changed their mind but didn't live through the attempt.

To illustrate this point, here is another case study. I worked with a family whose daughter struggled with severe and overwhelming depression. During her first semester of college, she had a depressive episode and was admitted to a psychiatric hospital. Eventually, she went back to her parents' home to recover. A month later, her mother walked in and found her unresponsive, with pink vomit splattered around her on the bathroom floor. The young woman was rushed to the hospital, where she had her stomach pumped and, fortunately, survived. Later, the parents found out their daughter's suicide attempt involved ingesting a large amount of pink antihistamine pills. After taking the medication, she changed her mind and tried to self-induce vomiting, but the sedating effects of the pills overwhelmed her. The next thing she remembered was waking up at the hospital. Luckily, she was discovered in time and began the road to recovery.

Myth 7: *People who attempt suicide have*
been planning it for days or months.

Often when someone makes an attempt, it's the result of what I call the *"perfect suicidal storm."* The person may have experienced thoughts of ending life for some time, but the actual decision to make an attempt was sudden and not well-planned-out. If you have experienced the wrath of a tornado, you know the environmental conditions must be near perfect for a tornado to manifest. Having grown up in Ohio and attended graduate school in Oklahoma, I know about this phenomenon all too well. Similarly, the perfect suicidal storm can involve a combination of factors: being under the influence of a substance(s), experiencing a high degree of distress or the effects of a traumatic event, feeling isolated, or lacking a support system. In these situations, the person is looking to escape a great deal of pain. And while some people plan out attempts for a longer period of time, this is not generally the case. People may enter that perfect storm suddenly, but there's a good possibility they can get out of it rather quickly as well.

To illustrate this point further, I had a client who was going through a divorce involving a custody battle over her son. She wasn't in contact with friends or family and was also experiencing high stress at work. One day, she was driving with a gun in her possession. She stopped and decided to call a suicide prevention hotline, in the hopes of being talked out of her plan. She relayed the situation to the staff member, telling them she had a gun and was having thoughts of ending her life. The staff member kept her talking long enough for police to trace the call. They found her pulled over on the side of the road. She was admitted to the hospital for evaluation and discharged after a few hours. The psychiatrist's assessment was that she was no longer in imminent danger of harming herself and had been going through acute stress. While there, she was honest about her mental and emotional state and didn't "play good" trying to get discharged. Of course, the police held onto the gun for a later return.

This was a good example of how a person can experience a combination of factors that causes them to contemplate suicide but can get back to a baseline of better functioning with some intervention or support. It's important to note that people who find themselves in a *"perfect suicidal storm"* must seek ongoing therapy and/or support to acquire tools to avoid these situations in the future. The more often people find themselves in this frame of mind, however fleeting, the increased likelihood they may move further toward making an attempt.

Myth 8: If I ask them about suicide, it will plant the idea in their minds.

Decades of research have found that asking people about their suicidality will not lead or influence them to attempt suicide. In fact, asking people struggling with suicidal thoughts may even help them become more open to talk about the pain they're enduring and the suffering that may be fueling their desire to harm or kill themselves. Don't beat around the bush when there is concern that someone may want to hurt themselves. Inquire directly from a caring place with questions such as, "Are you having thoughts of suicide/harming yourself/killing yourself?" Avoid leading or loaded questions, as it may alter the person's response. An example of a loaded question is, "You aren't wanting to harm yourself, are you?" "You want to live, yes?" "You are not having thoughts of dying, right?" If you suspect someone may be having suicidal ideation, it is imperative to be as direct as possible, but also caring. Approach the person in a validating, non-judgmental, and supportive manner. Also, if the person answers in the negative, claiming they do not have thoughts or intentions of harming themself, do not immediately take the response at face value. Make sure to follow up, especially if you suspect the person may be reticent about revealing their true thoughts due to concerns such as fear, shame, ridicule, judgment, or being hospitalized. Use your best judgment, and, if you are still concerned, seek help from a professional.

The Second Take Home:

Take all levels of suicidality seriously, even if a loved one may be using it as a form of manipulation, as this is not a healthy coping tool, and they will need to find healthier methods.

A possible response to someone having suicidality no matter the severity level:

"You sound very (insert emotion). You matter to me. I want to help you and wonder if you may need a higher level of care, or a professional to assist. Can we contact someone who can best help you? What can I do to help and support you?"

Must Know #11: Know the Other Potential Consequences of Untreated Mental Illness and Substance Abuse

What the Disease May Tell You

Your other kids must be coping well despite the chaos. They are getting good grades and staying out of trouble.

Your family seems to understand the great deal of time you commit helping Justin get better, despite the fact he's been struggling for the past five years.

You are strong and healthy. You seem to be handling the stress well, even after all of these years.

Why important:

When family members are not aware of additional consequences that may result when their struggling family member refuses to get help, the entire family can remain stuck in the same perpetual cycle of hurt, anger, and fear.

Sometimes family members are so engulfed by the fear of death that other, collateral effects are overlooked. Some of the ulterior consequences that can result when your struggling loved one doesn't get help are fracturing of the family unit, estrangement from loved ones, physical and emotional tolls, financial loss, etc. I've seen parents separate or divorce due to stress and differing views about how to approach their unwell family member (e.g., assertive love vs. enabling, stringent boundaries vs. softer boundaries, one last chance vs. no more chances). I have witnessed siblings take on a "hero" role (one who is doing all the "right things"), to offset the chaos and stress in the family. Often these siblings end up feeling lost, forgotten, or resentful. They might say, "My parents were so busy saving my brother, there was no time for me," "My kids don't know their grandparents, because they have been trying to help my sister for the past four decades," "I hate my brother for how much stress he caused the family. We watched my parents lose their livelihood over his refusal to get better."

When a family member remains untreated, consequences may result, such as potential harm to others. A daughter struggling with painkillers could fall asleep at the wheel and strike a family of pedestrians at a crosswalk. A son in a depressive episode may act out to harm others, due to his raging anger against society. Or a husband in an active, psychotic episode may see his wife as a diabolical entity and inflict harm on her to protect himself. Lastly, a young man selling drugs could find himself in a dangerous confrontation over money, and inadvertently harm innocent people.

Family members can also overlook the physical and emotional impact of an untreated family member's chronic disease on their own health. I worked with a mother in her eighties whose middle-aged daughter struggled with alcohol and had been in and out of treatment for two decades. The daughter's typical modus operandi was to check into a treatment center to make it "look good" to the judge after getting into legal trouble. Once the court appearance had passed, she'd prematurely discharge and return to drinking. Her mother enabled her with money and was fearful of setting boundaries. The stress became too much for the mother's heart, and she underwent quadruple bypass surgery. Afterward, she still wasn't willing to set boundaries and never got her daughter into ongoing treatment.

One more consequence should be mentioned and although it doesn't measure closely to the loss of a loved one, the dissolving of a marriage, or the ending of a family relationship, it is a reality many family members don't like to discuss—the financial toll. Usually, no one would dare to put a price tag on someone's health or wellbeing. As a culture, perhaps we believe this line of thinking is taboo, cold-hearted, or tone deaf. But I give families permission to talk about this reality out loud. Financial strain can severely impact health, relationships, and the future. The long-standing ordeal of paying for medical professionals, weekly therapy sessions, trips to the hospitals, ambulance rides to the emergency room, the fees associated with legal cases, multiple prior stints at treatment, etc., can add up to astonishing amounts. Sadly, I have heard grandparents discuss chipping away at their retirement to offset costs, parents delaying retirement or adding another job to pay the bills, families taking out loans to pay for treatment or borrowing money to support the recovery process.

Families need to understand that the financial support they've been contributing to support their loved one's perpetual struggles pales in comparison to what a treatment program and after-care for a year would cost. So, allow yourselves to talk about issues you feel might be socially inappropriate with your health care professionals or therapists. Staying silent about various consequences is exactly what the disease wants you to do—leave it alone, not talk about it, and not take action against it.

> **The Take Home:**
>
> Be mindful about the collateral consequences of untreated mental health and substance use, as many other people aside from your struggling loved ones can be impacted.

Must Know #12: Know the Disease Does Not Define Anyone—So, Know Not to Underestimate Your Loved Ones' Insight and Awareness

What the Disease May Tell You

There's no way Eli has any sense of what he is doing. He is schizophrenic.

Shanice is too depressed to make any decisions for herself.

Gerald is an opiate user, and he'll never have the capacity to get a job.

Alexis' bipolar disorder basically means she can never have a normal life, as she will be in and out of hospitals.

> **Why important:**
>
> Too often, family members don't realize the disease is a separate entity, and they fail to recognize their untreated loved one's strengths and capabilities. In the same vein, the unwell person doesn't recognize they have strengths that can help them through the struggle, and that the disease does not define them.

As I mentioned earlier, loving family members may unintentionally enable when trying to help from a loving place. They may also enable because they are fearful of deleterious outcomes such as death. When families are paralyzed by fear, the untreated person begins to act according to what they may feel are the thought and behavior patterns appropriate for their diagnoses. For example, if someone is diagnosed with schizophrenia, they may believe they can't ever change. The family may conclude the loved one is incapable of living a healthy life or taking on bigger career responsibilities. They may unwittingly project onto them a limited scope for a productive future because of the perception that the person is not capable of getting better. Family members might treat the person according to their symptoms and overlook their strengths and capabilities. When you predominantly treat someone according to symptoms of their disease (e.g., lack of motivation, mood instability, social isolation, intellectual disability) and fail to recognize their other attributes (e.g., talents, skills, abilities), they begin to define themselves as the disease and limit their daily lives by these lower-level expectations.

Allow me to cite a few real-life scenarios to illustrate this idea. My first example was a daughter who was involuntarily admitted to the hospital due to certain risk behaviors towards herself and others (e.g., cutting herself, talking about dying, and having auditory hallucinations). Family members feared for their safety and were no longer able to care for her. This was her third hospital visit in eight months, and she knew how to finagle the system to get discharged. As long as she showered, consumed the food they gave her, denied wanting to harm herself, and didn't exhibit psychotic features, she would be discharged. After forty-eight hours in the hospital, the attending psychiatrist visited with her. The patient denied any desires to harm herself (although she still had plans to do so) and convinced him she was no longer hearing voices (although she still was). As a result, she was discharged. In this case, she'd had enough self and environmental awareness and insight to display behaviors she knew were conducive to healthier living. Even those severely impaired usually have a level of insight to enable conscious decisions and the ability to differentiate between appropriate and inappropriate behaviors.

My second example was a grandson who struggled with heroin and was unable to carry on a conversation or apply for a single job. He couldn't follow through with chores and lacked the ability to make his own meals. With only a dollar to his name, no car, and no phone, he found out where to score free black tar heroin seventy miles from his grandparents' home. Somehow, he made it there in record time. Again, this is an example where we might have underestimated one's capabilities, or not recognized one's capacities. But when true desire is present, people can go above and beyond expectations—no matter how impaired they may be.

I am hoping these examples help get the point across. Time and time again, family members use "porcelain gloves" being overly delicate in their approaches, fearful of the worst outcomes and not realizing that their struggling family members have more insight and abilities than they thought. Families need to understand the disease affects their loved ones but does not define who they are. Just as someone with diabetes would not introduce themselves by saying, "Hi, I am diabetes," I would never encourage someone to say, "Hi, I am schizophrenia." If the topic came up in conversation, I would encourage a response such as, "I struggle (or am diagnosed with or have) schizophrenia." Not recognizing a person's full abilities or defining them by their diagnoses further perpetuates their struggle and can prevent the ability to pull themselves up to a place where they can get help. Instead, give them the guidance to tap into the belief that they still have what it takes to fight back.

The Take Home:

Know that your loved ones are more capable than you think, however sick or impaired you think they may be. Don't allow the disease to define them, and don't allow them to define themselves as the disease!

Must Know #13: Know to Recognize that Change Can Emerge from Desperation (Let Go of the Emotional Tug-of-War)

What the Disease May Tell You

> *You're cruel to keep Jose out of his home because he refuses to be sober. He is going to die out there.*
>
> *How could you not give money to your granddaughter, Leticia, when she begs you? Maybe she uses some of it for marijuana and occasional hallucinogens, but at least she can get meals.*
>
> *You'd rather your son, Deshaun, be locked in a psychiatric hospital with sick people because he verbally threatens you, rather than let him stay at home, where he can be comfortable, and you can watch over him?*

> **Why important:**
>
> Putting your family member into a heightened level of desperation is very unnatural to what you know as a loving family unit. This discomfort prevents you from taking the necessary actions to get help and allows them to continue in their unhealthy states.

Earlier, I likened the disease to an adversary or opponent. We need to respect its capabilities, anticipate its next move, manage its power, and outsmart it. The biggest strength of any disease is the ability to survive by creating options to thrive. For instance, a rat can squeeze through a hole the size of a dime to get away or survive. Visualize the disease as a mouse finding a way to escape a maze. It will go through any opening, even if it means squeezing through the smallest fissures. Similarly, the disease is always on the move, looking for ways to get away, thrive, and remain undiscovered. The only way to trap the mouse is to completely shut off every opportunity to get away, which is what families need to do—shut down all options for the disease to maneuver.

When families have been trying to get help for their loved ones, providing too many options is an area of focus. Some examples of unproductive options may be a grandparent who regularly gives her unwell family member money when in need, a friend who offers a place to stay when your loved one is homeless, or siblings loaning vehicles when the loved one loses the capability to drive. When shutting these outlets down, remember to use assertive love rather than tough love. Assertive love encompasses the balance between rules and relationships. Essentially, you can still love, empathize, and show compassion towards your loved ones, while setting limits to get them help. We need to reframe our typical responses into a new approach, one with clearer boundaries and firmer messages.

Call this strategy "Setting up your loved one to a point of desperation." Some may refer to this desperation point as "rock bottom." According to Collins English Dictionary, *desperation* is "the feeling you have when you are in such a bad situation that you will try anything to change it." Similar to the aims of tough love, the intention behind forcing rock bottom is well-meaning. The challenge lies in the possibility of misinterpretation by some families. The essence of rock bottom is allowing the unwell ones to struggle until they "bottom out" and can no longer dig deeper. Some examples of this rock bottom place may be when the loved one is no longer capable of working and earning a living, when family has stopped offering support, or when they become homeless, incarcerated, or in the hospital. Sometimes, families think forcing rock bottom means cutting all ties, but if this happens, your untreated member may believe everyone has given up and they are completely on their own. This mindset can lead to hopelessness, which can lead to a higher risk of suicidality.

As I mentioned earlier, the instillation of hope is critical for both family members and the person struggling. Sometimes I doubt whether those who experience long-term homelessness, either in active psychosis or while severely impaired, can discern what rock bottom looks like from a health perspective. These same people, however, will still have a degree of awareness and insight into what desperation may feel like (e.g., hunger, physical suffering, lack of financial means, etc.). With this type of desperation, they will want to do anything to relieve the pain. The strategy is to let your loved ones know there are other ways to alleviate suffering, but the family will no longer support unhealthy means. Knowing that family members are waiting in the trenches if they decide to seek help instills hope and possibility. They realize their families are waiting with open arms for them to abandon their unhealthy lifestyle. Furthermore, the perception that there is a support system (e.g., family) available if needed (even if the loved one is estranged from the support system) tends to maintain hope, compared to the perception that there is no support.

This limiting approach constricts any options not conducive to a path of healthier living. It does not tell your unwell family members when they *can't* do something (e.g., not use drugs or refuse psychiatric medications); a "forcing the hand" approach does not yield great results and often turns into a power struggle. The "you have options" approach communicates clearly what the choices are and assures family support if they choose the healthier route. This strategy also prevents an emotional tug-of-war by eliminating the perception that it's "my way or the highway." I believe whenever you communicate that someone has no choice in a matter, resistance is likely.

Furthermore, whenever someone is forced into a state of desperation, a fight, flight, or freeze response results. For example, a human who has not eaten a morsel of food for an extended period of time will likely consume near anything, no matter how unappetizing it may be, as a means to survive. Perhaps, we've all reached a point in our lives when we have felt desperate, whether it be financially, medically, or emotionally. At these moments of desperation, we'd do almost anything to make the situation better. We can fight (take the situation head on and search for solutions), take flight (avoid the situation altogether and hope it miraculously works itself out), or freeze (become paralyzed to the point of inaction). Both fight and freeze are good places for your untreated family members to be, because with fight, people are nearing a state of readiness to make the changes to get better. And in a state of freeze, people are generally left with few or no options when seeking help is their last resort to making the situation better. Flight can only last for so long. Sooner or later, it'll come to an end, as long as family members no longer prolong the flight process by giving more paths and options (e.g., money and resources).

When I coach families about setting up their loved one to a point of desperation, we work on identifying the options on the table perpetuating their loved one's unhealthy lifestyle (e.g., paying for an apartment, providing allowance, borrowing a car, etc.). Of course, families are understandably fraught with fear and guilt, knowing they will have to communicate to their unwell family members that support will be rescinded. This concept is foreign to families who have been lending support for years. Some typical statements are, "You're telling us you want us to kick our daughter out of the house?" "If I stop giving my brother money, how is he going to eat?" "We are asked to stop paying rent and providing an allowance, so my grandson will be homeless?" My response to these families is, "No, I am asking you to tell your loved ones they have options. They are more than welcome to live their current lifestyle, but you are no longer going to support it. You will only support a lifestyle conducive to healthier living. You will always love and support them, but you won't support their unhealthy path any longer."

Recall what I said earlier about the importance of giving people the ability to choose. My strategy is for family members to be very clear about which options they will support moving forward. My *Must Know #15* will explain what those options are, which I refer to as "The Non-Negotiables." Remember, this approach is not a cold-hearted, draconian measure, but one of understanding, compassion, and care—yet with clear boundaries and expectations. Using assertive love is a key part of the strategy.

Here is a case that effectively illustrates the importance of limiting options to a point of desperation. The case involved a family who sought my help for their grandson. He was the eldest of three siblings, and his parents were deceased. His father had been his grandparents' only child. The grandparents were successful entrepreneurs, and under their care, the grandson had done well academically. But he'd been diagnosed with a psychiatric condition, and the symptoms made it hard for him to keep jobs or make sound career decisions. Up to that point, he had refused to seek treatment. The grandparents had plans for the grandson to take over the family business, a decision in line with their culture's norms, which provided that the eldest son or grandson assume the family estate and business. They were deeply concerned that if their grandson didn't get help, he'd put the business at risk and the estate would be vulnerable. Plus, his psychotic symptoms were worsening, and he'd had a few run-ins with the police as a result of his erratic behaviors. The grandparents were older and knew they wouldn't be able to run the business for much longer.

I learned they'd also been giving the grandson a six-figure monetary amount at the start of each new year as capital to start his own business. The grandson wanted to prove that he could take over the family business and also create his own successful company from the ground up, with some help to get started. The grandparents paid for his apartment and credit cards, provided an ample monthly allowance, and had purchased three cars. The first thing I asked them was, "How do I sign up to be your grandson?" On a more serious note, I asked, "Where is the motivation for him to get help and change his lifestyle?"

Essentially, they needed to set him up for desperation. They agreed to suspend the yearly salary, stop paying for credit cards, bills, and his apartment, cease the monthly allowance, and stop purchasing cars for him, as long as he refused to get help for his condition. After three months, the grandson was completely out of money, facing an eviction notice, and maxed out on his credit cards. After being homeless for a few days, he was taken to the hospital. The distress of being homeless was unbearable, so he chose the option to get treatment.

This case example shows the power of limiting options and putting a person who refuses help into a state of desperation. The untreated person learned that his relatives would support him, provided he sought treatment. The message was clear: the family would no longer support an unhealthy lifestyle.

> **The Take Home:**
>
> Limiting options is an effective strategy to get your loved one closer to surrendering and reaching a place of desperation to accept help. Put down the emotional, tug-of-war rope!

Must Know #14: Know to Recognize the Leverage(s)

What the Disease May Tell You

Nothing will change Tony's mind about taking care of his depression.

If you stop paying for Alejandra's apartment, it will only fuel her anger, and she will never want anything to do with you.

Not even Nick's own kids can get him to change his unhealthy lifestyle.

> **Why important:**
>
> When family members begin to feel hopeless and powerless about the chronic situation, they have more power than they may think to get their struggling ones help. This defeated mindset delays the start of the treatment and recovery processes.

Whenever I meet families struggling to get their untreated family members into treatment, one of the most critical pieces of information I gather is what leverages they have. Leverages are people, places, or things deemed important by the unwell person that can influence their decisions. Examples of leverages can be financial support, housing, transportation, employment, paying for schooling, and maintaining relationships.

Remember, you are not taking these supports away, you are simply setting a boundary; if they do not move towards a healthier path of living, the family will remove these aspects of support. If the loved ones decide to get help and manage their condition(s), the family will happily recommence support.

Please note, I don't advocate using relationships or children as a primary means of leverage; in some cases, families resort to this option out of a desperate need for help. One prominent example was a client who struggled with methamphetamines, substance-induced psychosis, depression, and anger fits. He had displayed aggressive behavior towards his wife during meth-induced rages, and she'd been forced to attain a restraining order to protect her and their five kids. As a result, he became homeless for a few months. The client loved his kids dearly and was distraught he could not be with them. The wife informed him she would consider revising the restraining order when he was sober for at least one year, consistently taking psychiatric medications, and seeing a therapist. The desire to be back together with his kids forced him to start treatment and begin the path to recovery. Had his wife allowed him to see the kids without getting help, the likelihood of his seeking treatment would have been greatly diminished. To him, it would have been the best of both worlds—using substances and carrying on an unhealthy lifestyle while still being part of his children's lives. Again, I would never advise families to utilize relationships or kids as a source of leverage and would explore other options first, but even relationships (e.g., spousal, child(ren), parental, peer) can be a powerful tool to get unwell ones to make necessary changes in their lives.

> **The Take Home:**
>
> Identify the powerful leverages that will be strong influences in getting your loved ones help.

Must Know #15: Know to Stay Strong and Insist on the Non-Negotiables

What the Disease May Tell You

> *Rafael does not need a psychiatrist for his anxiety and depression. They will just drug him up and make him a zombie.*
> *What's a little marijuana going to do? It will probably help Nina calm down the voices. Medications aren't going to do too much for his obsessive-compulsive disorder (OCD), Ali just needs to avoid thinking about things too much.*

> **Why important:**
>
> Family members often lack a unified vision when it comes to upholding the non-negotiables, which ends up prolonging their untreated ones' struggles.

Having coached so many families, I believe working to narrow down options is a critical step in the boundary-setting stage. It is important to note the options must be well-considered, specific, realistic, manageable and reasonable in number, or the loved one will feel overwhelmed, and that family support is unattainable. Remember, the goal is to get them into the first phase of the treatment process. We are not considering longer-term goals at this early juncture, such as securing a home, getting a full-time job, or becoming financially autonomous. These very important goals are more appropriate in the later phases of the treatment process when stabilization is occurring. I will address these broader goals in more depth in Chapters 7 and 9.

In the pre-treatment phase, I tell families there are three non-negotiables (and three other contingencies) their unwell ones absolutely need to accept and adopt.

Non-negotiables:

1. Practice absolute and continual abstinence from *all illicit, non-prescribed* mind-altering substances (Please recall, I discuss harm reduction in Chapter 6 as a potential option).
2. Be under the care of a psychiatric medical provider.
3. Take all medications (if needed) as prescribed

Important but Negotiable:

4. Enter a treatment program.
5. Sign a Release of Information to speak to providers.
6. See a therapist/counselor for counseling.

Numbers 1-3 are deal-breakers because they assume the struggling family members are at a severe stage and the use of mind-altering substances is not conducive to a healthy path of recovery. This includes marijuana, opiates (unless indicated and under close medical supervision), and even attention-deficit hyperactivity disorder (ADHD) medications (if stimulant form and unless also indicated under close medical supervision). Further, it's assumed the loved one is in an acute, severe state and psychiatric medications would help move them towards a healthier baseline level of functioning. Please note, if substance use is part of their struggles or history, I highly recommend seeking a psychiatric medical provider who specializes or works with addiction patients.

The fourth item, entering a treatment program, is considered a possibility rather than a non-negotiable because a formal treatment program may not be fully necessary at the current time, if their struggles are not severe. In this case, numbers one to three, along with some form of counseling, may be effective. However, as I mentioned in the introduction, most family members reading this book are most likely in acute crisis, and their untreated ones are severe enough to require intensive treatment. Whether a treatment program is necessary should be determined with a psychiatric medical provider and/or a mental health professional.

The fifth item on the list, the release of information, is extremely important but shouldn't be a deal breaker. Release of Information is when a patient (presumably an adult) provides consent for providers to speak about his/her case to others. The patient typically is specific about who this information can be shared with (e.g., family members, spouse, other providers, place of work, etc.) along with the extent of the information details (e.g., only diagnoses/ medications/ frequency of appointments, or no restrictions at all). If families can get their unwell family members to agree to this one, great. If not, perhaps they can agree to it further along the treatment process. I include this on the list because sometimes those struggling are not transparent about their symptoms, forthright about their struggle, or clear about their clinical histories. Allowing family members to speak to providers can circumvent any misinformation or fill in any shortage of critical details about the best way to create the treatment plan. So, having them sign a release of information is important at some point.

Please note, if your loved one does not consent for you to speak to their providers, it doesn't mean you can't submit information. The provider won't be able to confirm or speak to you about any aspects of meetings or treatment, but this notion of submitting information can also be used for courts and attorneys. I have recommended family members submit a letter to a judge or district attorney, giving a contextual understanding of the case and perhaps, requesting their family member be assigned to mental health court or allowed to negotiate treatment instead of a jail or prison sentence. I have witnessed cases in which judges and district attorneys have agreed to such a proposal, and the struggling persons have been able to seek treatment and avoid incarceration. Lastly, I have found the court system to be increasingly receptive to treatment as a viable alternative, especially if the person is a first-time violator and/or recidivism (recommitting a crime) is less likely with treatment.

As a provider, I always appreciated typed-out letters, emails, or conversations to help understand the full spectrum of what the clients are navigating. Clients—especially younger ones or those who are impaired—are not always the best self-historians. However, be mindful of this approach, as your loved one may lose trust in you, the provider, and the process itself if they learn you are communicating without their awareness. At times, the situation is so desperate that this measure validates the risk and supersedes any collateral concerns. When your loved one gets better, they will realize you were acting from a loving place and attempting to get them help.

The sixth item on the list requires your unwell member to see a therapist or counselor, but I do not recommend it as a deal-breaker. If they agree to therapy, that is great progress. If they don't right away, perhaps they may reconsider once they gain a little time in sobriety, stabilization from medications, or are less acute in their mental health struggles. At some point in the future, they may be more motivated and clear-minded about seeking extra support. Forcing them into therapy during their heightened acuities may turn into a power struggle, or they may feel pushed to the wall and forced to talk to someone, especially if they are not in the mental space to trust others and make self-disclosures. If they choose to be in therapy, we want them to feel it's a safe place to talk and work with someone on their issues. A competent therapist will be able to assess whether the person is being dishonest or engaging in behaviors that put them at immediate risk. Remember, therapists are mandatory reporters and have to report if a client is in imminent danger of harming themselves or others or is gravely disabled, or if child or elderly abuse is suspected.

The Take Home:

Understand the non-negotiables as critical elements in boundary-setting and no-exception options for your loved ones if they are to receive your support.

Must Know #16: Know to Drain the Weakened Battery and Limited Gas Tank

What the Disease May Tell You

> *Gianna can go on forever with this dangerous lifestyle. She has been doing it for so long, there is no point trying to change her.*
>
> *How is ten dollars enabling Curtis? What can he do with such a small amount of money?*
>
> *Couch surfing with friends is harmless. At least Natalie has a place to sleep at night.*

Why important:

People who are struggling with this powerful disease can exist for a long time with very little support, and even small, incremental aid hinders them from getting necessary help.

If you recall, earlier I talked about the reason why affected people continue to engage in the same unhealthy patterns of behaviors for a long period of time—*because they can!* And, as we have been discussing, a few ways to hinder their downward spiral are to limit options, set boundaries, and follow through with the non-negotiables.

Maybe you are at the point where your family has done their part holding boundaries and accepting the three inevitable consequences—hospital, jail, death—but your struggling ones haven't gotten to the point of asking for help. It feels like an endless waiting game. Now what?

All of us have a maximum threshold or breaking point at which we cannot go on any longer. This max point is the utmost capacity we can deal with something. Some examples can be the level of emotional stress a person can manage until the stress becomes unbearable, the amount of weight one can lift in the gym before they cannot do any more repetitions, the number of miles a person can run before cramping, or the array of job tasks a person can handle before performance decreases. My point is, we all have a threshold, a finite battery life or a limited gas tank.

This same breaking point is even more pronounced for your unwell family members once they have no options on the table and all leverages are being withheld until they agree to seek help. The goal is for them to reach a level of sheer desperation and realize help is the only option. In most cases, those in acute crisis with little-to-no resources have a low threshold, comparatively speaking, to someone with more resources and support. Sooner rather than later, the sicker they become from not getting help, they'll find themselves in increasingly precarious situations that may inevitably involve jail, hospital, or homelessness. From that point, getting help may be the only remaining alternative.

Speaking of desperation, we can all relate to having two percent battery life on our cell phones when we're expecting an important call. Of course, this always happens on the one day we forget our charger at home. We feel anxious, worried, and desperate. Our phone is showing one red bar, so we borrow a friend's charger for five minutes. Our phone gets to fifteen percent, and a sense of temporary relief comes over us. We now have a few yellow bars and are in the clear for another hour or so.

This analogy has real-life implications for your untreated family members who are out there, not functioning on a full battery yet able to get an occasional charge. Attaining a slight recharge prolongs their ability to sustain their current way of living. Some of the ways family members provide a little charge or put gas in a struggling person's tank can be depositing a few dollars each week on their debit cards for food, getting them a hotel room a day or two a week, putting fuel in their car, or paying credit card balances, allowing them more spendable credit to use. Often families rationalize their actions by saying, "I'm only giving a few dollars," or "We aren't letting him stay at home but do get a motel room on occasion." My response is that although you are not giving much, you are providing enough support to keep them going at the bare minimum. As I said earlier, the untreated person in acute crisis still has a degree of insight and awareness, and they can do a lot with few resources (recall my example of having the $1 dollar in the pocket but still being able to travel to score free drugs). The goal is to completely drain the battery or empty the tank, so they are only left with the fight, flight, or freeze responses.

One example was an uncle and aunt who came to see me regarding their middle-aged nephew, who was struggling with his mental health and substance use. The nephew had income from his contract job moving homes and would travel to multiple cities around the surrounding counties. He was struggling with depression, drinking alcohol, and nearing homelessness, but the moving job allowed him enough income to rent rooms several times a week. The uncle and aunt were concerned, as he had increasingly exhibited bizarre behaviors. They were worried he may have untreated bipolar disorder and psychosis due to his manic symptoms. The extended family was large, and he had up to thirty cousins in the surrounding areas he could stay with throughout the year. I advised them to shut down all of the options on the table. The uncle sent out a mass email to the extended family members, asking them to redirect the nephew back to them and not allow him to stay over or provide him with money or food. The uncle also spoke to the owner of the moving company, who was not happy his employee was working while intoxicated. The owner told the nephew he had to get help for his drinking problem and agree to random drug screening. With no money or places to stay, and after one month of homelessness, the nephew agreed to enter treatment and get sober. Essentially, his battery life surviving on his own devices ran out.

The Take Home:

Do whatever you can to drain the battery life and empty your loved one's gas tank. A bare minimum of resources can sustain them. Once they are nearly or completely tapped out of resources, you can maximize their chances of reaching a heightened level of desperation, which will leave them with no option other than agreeing to treatment if they want change.

Must Know #17: Know That Some of the Worst Places to End Up Can Be the Best Places to End Up

What the Disease May Tell You

You are so mean not to bail Maritza out of jail. Do you know how much danger she can be in?

How can you send Bradley straight to treatment after the hospitalization?

He is probably scared and will be too fearful to ever harm himself again.

I understand she is refusing to get help for her bipolar disorder, but letting Riva live at random friends' homes is so dangerous. Wouldn't she be safer in her own room at your house?

> **Why important:**
>
> Families often harbor so much fear about where their untreated family members may end up, that they are too scared to take the necessary steps to get them help. This can lead to their loved ones suffering more inevitable consequences.

As parents, we could never imagine as we held our little ones as infants and stared into their innocent eyes that one day they could be locked up in jail, admitted to a mental health hospital, homeless, or more heart-wrenchingly, deceased before we are.

However, these unfathomable consequences (excluding death) may be the best places your severely impaired loved ones can end up, as it increases the chances of them getting help. Family members have told me that while their struggling ones were in prison or the mental health hospital, they slept better than they had in ages. This sense of relief came from having their loved one in a secured location and being cared for. All in all, there was less risk for harm, compared to when their loved one was on the streets in extreme distress.

Moreover, in nearly ninety percent of the clients I have worked with, being homeless, incarcerated, or in a mental health hospital is not a sustainable situation, which is why these are good sources of desperation points where leverages can be most effective. Some people can thrive in incarceration or remain homeless for years, but again, these people are outliers. Even in these rare cases, there is a threshold at which they'd rather be anywhere else.

By the way, when I say "homeless," I am not referring to couch surfing at friends' homes, living in personal campers, or driving across the country in minivans. When I refer to true homelessness, I am talking about sleeping under bridges, residing behind or in abandoned buildings, napping on bus benches while begging for money on street corners, or dumpster diving for food. The reason I accentuate this concept is because it brings to mind two cases (among many) that validate my hypothesis of how most people cannot endure true homelessness.

First was a young, muscular male who presented to treatment with a history of amphetamine abuse, anger, untreated psychiatric conditions, a series of physical altercations, and various brief stints in jail. One day, he was fed up with treatment and wanted to leave. His parents did not support his departure and refused to purchase a plane ticket for his return home. Nonetheless, he was hard set on discharging. After multiple redirections from staff, he demanded his belongings, adamant about pawning some of his stuff to make it "on the outside." A few hours later, evening hit, it began to rain lightly, and he returned to treatment. He said he didn't like the rain and cold (not to mention the tough streets of—hint of sarcasm—the beach area of south Orange County, California).

The second example was a young female I worked with who struggled with mental health and marijuana abuse and had lost her ability to live at home due to her parents' boundary setting. She decided to try to make it on the streets selling drugs across the border. That fantasy came to a quick end when local gang members told her to "Leave town or else…"

Incarceration can also be a powerful situation compelling your unwell family member into treatment. I met a family whose adult daughter struggled with alcoholism. They were extremely worried she might die or accidentally kill someone due to her dangerous behaviors when intoxicated. A few weeks later, she had a car accident and was arrested for driving under the influence (DUI). Luckily, no one was injured. The father called me and asked if he should bail her out. We decided it would be best if she remained in jail until released by the courts. In the meantime, the parents made it clear that she could not return home until she completed a treatment program for substance abuse after her release. Knowing she had nowhere to go and after some time in jail to re-examine her life's trajectory, she agreed to treatment and remained on a path of recovery. Moreover, another powerful leverage can be when loved ones have a probation or parole officer, and incarceration is a situation they want to avoid at all costs. In those cases, when the client begins to resist treatment, a quick reminder that their probation or parole officer may receive a phone call gets them quickly back on track.

This same approach also works for those admitted into psychiatric units. I've had clients who experienced both incarceration and mental health hospitalizations, and some have noted that jail was less distressful and preferable. Again, in situations when your unwell family members have been hospitalized on a temporary hold, it is vital to inform them they cannot return directly home but rather, must enter a treatment program for ongoing care.

Conservatorship/guardianship/power of attorney

It is also important to note that after multiple psychiatric hospitalizations, your adult loved one may be considered for a court-appointed conservatorship, which is when another adult is granted legal rights over certain aspects of an incapacitated adult's life (e.g., financial affairs). With the help of the treating psychiatrist in the hospital and a case worker, you can request a county-assigned conservator or be the conservator yourself, though I highly recommend the former, if possible, due to the multiple roles (i.e., parental, conservator, payee, etc.) the designated family members will have to take on. Having conservatorship allows a great deal of leverage in getting help or moving them towards a level of desperation (e.g., limit financial access), and can serve as a protective measure if problems arise again in the future.

Sometimes, the conservatorship process is effective in getting help but can also create challenges in relationships. A noteworthy example is one between an adult and his parent, who served as conservator after his mental health crisis. The conservatorship allowed his parent to oversee his medical care and financial dealings. Through intensive treatment, he was eventually able to stabilize and attain a healthy baseline of functioning. However, over time, what was initially an effective set-up presented challenges, as his parent found herself taking on multiple roles (i.e., parent, grandparent, conservator).

Another option that family members may explore is guardianship. This court-appointed arrangement grants an adult legal right over both the financial matters and well-being (i.e., medical care) of a minor. Guardianship also encompasses the legal right to oversee and decide the medical needs of the person in need (conservatorship typically focuses on financial affairs). Additionally, conservatorship is geared towards an adult loved one, while the guardianship is for minors.

Last, power of attorney is a "legally binding document" that a person (e.g., your unwell loved one) assigns another person or entity to manage their financial, property, or medical affairs. This arrangement is not court-appointed and the person who appointed the designated person or entity to serve in this role may rescind or revise the agreement at any time.

Contact your family attorney, social worker, or psychiatrist for additional guidance on any of these options if it is deemed necessary as a strategic avenue to attain necessary care for your loved one. All these options have their advantages and disadvantages and it's best to consult with professionals for additional direction.

I highlight these stories and mention these options for leverage to illustrate that although homelessness, incarceration, or hospitalizations are not circumstances we'd ever want for our loved ones, each can be an effective means to get them closer to treatment. These unwanted situations and/or arrangements can warp-speed a level of desperation and set them up for getting help.

The Take Home:

Incarcerations, hospitalizations, or temporary homelessness can, ironically, be favorable situations for your loved ones, as it positions them at a point of desperation where surrendering and getting help are the only viable options.

Must Know #18: Know to Prioritize the Healthy Track Record, not Legal, Academic, or Credit Score Records

What the Disease May Tell You

If you stop paying Meredith's credit cards, she'll never be able to reclaim her good credit.

If you call the police on Max, he will have a record, completely ruining any chances for getting his dream job.

If you don't pay Pierre's rent, he'll be evicted. He'll never be able to buy a car, rent an apartment, or purchase a home in the future due to his ruined credit score.

Why important:

Sometimes family members lose focus of the most important priorities and worry about less critical consequences not linked to saving their struggling ones' lives.

Besides the fear of losing an untreated member, there are other reasons why families are resistant to taking the necessary actions to get help. The most prominent reasons involve aspects that may impact their future such as legal records, academic pursuits, and credit ratings. All are important, but not as important as safety and health.

Again, family members are mostly well-intentioned, doing what they can to protect and preserve the untreated person's future. But sometimes, they miss the picture of what is most important in the here and now. Run-ins with the legal system, failing grades on a school transcript, and a poor credit score all have future implications. But these distant, secondary outcomes won't matter if their unwell family members are deceased, incarcerated for life, severely impaired or catastrophically injured as a result of their untreated substance use and mental health struggles. All these issues are repairable; lost lives are not.

As I mentioned earlier, we, as parents, would never want to put our loved ones in a position to fail, but sometimes family members need to take necessary actions to get them help. For instance, having a police record may actually provide leverage, if the police end up arresting your unwell family member after too many run-ins, thereby leading to a court order that requires agreement to treatment or facing incarceration. If a family stops paying on a credit card, it may negatively impact your loved one's credit scores, so they are no longer able to use them, acquire other credit cards, or apply for loans. Limiting their access to money or other resources can move them towards a point of desperation.

I am a big believer in allowing people to experience the natural consequences of their behaviors and decisions (to a reasonable degree). This model can be applied to nearly any area of life, from a parent compelling a fifth-grade boy to be responsible and bring his homework to school, to a senior executive training a mid-level manager to run team meetings or to a Jiu-Jitsu coach teaching a student to properly defend from an arm bar submission. If the fifth grader repeatedly forgets his homework but his dad drops it off at the school each time, the boy won't face the natural consequences (e.g., lower grade) for his inattentiveness to his responsibilities. If the senior manager keeps chiming in whenever the manager-in-training gets stumped during team meetings, the trainee will never become autonomous and work through his discomforts. Lastly, if the Jiu-Jitsu coach doesn't allow the student to get caught in a submission move, the student will never discover how to defend against it. This same approach is effective for people resisting help with their substance use or mental health condition. Facing the natural consequences of their actions and behaviors can move them toward a point of desperation, and that low point may be the impetus needed for growth and change.

Calling law enforcement

Please remember, if you or your family members ever feel in imminent danger from threats or actions of your affected one, never hesitate to call the police. It's imperative to know that when you do call, the language you use can potentially impact the type of response you may receive from first responders. If the goal is to get your loved one into treatment, the content of your call is essential. If your loved one is acting out by damaging property, using threatening language or acting erratically, and you say, "My son is out of control and damaging our home," the law enforcement agency will most likely respond as if it's a domestic disturbance/violence call, one of the most potentially dangerous calls they receive. The language I recommend using instead is, *"My son has an untreated mental health issue and may be a danger to himself and others."* This latter wording will be approached as a mental health case, and the first responders may even arrive accompanied by a local mental health evaluation team to assess the need for hospitalization. Some law enforcement agencies are increasingly adding mental health training to their curriculum. The first call mentioned above may inspire a different type of vigilance and put your loved ones at greater risk to be injured or even killed, as domestic calls can be dangerous and, in some cases, deadly for law enforcement officers. The second response will let the officers know they'll be dealing with someone mentally unstable who may need higher-level care. It's still a potentially dangerous scenario for the officers, but the lens through which they will assess your struggling family member may be different. It's also important to inform law enforcement if there are any weapons in the home, or if your loved one is acting aggressively or experiencing psychosis.

The Take Home:

Focus on the urgency of saving your loved ones' lives when making decisions to get them help. Worrying about consequences less critical to their health and safety (e.g., legal implications, financial or career loss) will delay getting them the help they truly need.

Must Know #19: Know to Keep Planting the Emotional Seeds

What the Disease May Tell You

Nothing you say matters to Kamal. He doesn't care about your love.

Those voicemails telling Iris you love her are falling on deaf ears. Leo wants nothing to do with the family and wouldn't care if any of you were in his life.

Why important:

At times, families forget to show their unwell family members they are still loved, which can lead to hopelessness when they believe no one cares for them.

So, you've done everything you can to make it clear to your loved one what options are available to attain your support. You've limited non-productive options, set them up for desperation, and held strong to the non-negotiables. Now, what can you do in the interim? Some common questions I receive from families at this juncture are, "How can we support them emotionally?" "Why do we feel so powerless?" "Is there any way we can still express our love, so they won't think we gave up on them?"

As mentioned earlier, I advise family members at this stage to keep "planting the emotional seeds." These seeds can be texts telling the affected person you're thinking of them and praying for their good health, voicemails expressing your love and the hope they will get help and rejoin the family, or letters letting them know you will be waiting for them when they turn things around and finally accept help.

One man I worked with in treatment told me he regretted the emotional pain he had caused his mom while he was out using drugs and making her stay up all night worrying. Throughout that time, she would continually send texts telling him she was praying for his safety and thinking about him every day. She'd say she hoped he'd get better soon so they could be together again. He said these texts had meant a lot to him during treatment, though her messages were the ultimate "buzz kill" when he was thinking about getting high. At his point of pure desperation, these messages gave him the motivation to get better, because he finally realized there were people in the world he was hurting, and he still wanted to be a part of their lives. Had it not been for those texts, he wasn't sure whether he'd be alive today.

You may recall that earlier I discussed the dangers of harboring hopelessness, and how it correlates to suicidality. One way to instill hope in your loved ones, even if they are desperate and resisting help, is by planting these emotional seeds. Just as the mother above passed on messages to her son that conveyed unrelenting, unconditional love, planting seeds with your loved one will remind them during brief moments of clarity that people care for them. This may be enough to validate their life is still worth fighting for.

When people believe others in the world love and support them, their chances of getting help are greater than those who feel alone, even if the latter is not actually the case. People who believe they have no one to rely on also have a greater risk of giving up on life (e.g., suicidality) than those who believe loving people continue to care for them—a huge factor in instilling hope.

The Take Home:

Know the power in planting emotional seeds, even at the height of your loved ones' struggles. These seeds may be a deciding factor to fight and germinate at the moment of desperation as they contemplate reasons to get help.

Must Know #20: Know "We're Done" and "I'm Done" Can Be Music to the Ears

What the Disease May Tell You

Even if he doesn't want to get healthy, if you stop helping Isaiah now, it's a death sentence.

Selena needs money to survive, so why stop supporting her just because she refuses to take medication?

Jacob will never give up his alcohol. It is the only way for him to function and survive.

Why important:

Sometimes, families get caught up in complex verbal exchanges, not recognizing that short, clear phrases are most effective in getting their point across to untreated family members.

Sometimes, the most profound messages we can communicate or receive are short, to the point, and clear—and this type of message should be used when trying to get help for your affected ones.

I often advise family members that the statement "We are done" is complete and clear, especially for those families who have been struggling to get their loved ones help for a long time but lacked follow-through on boundary setting. When you use this statement with your struggling loved one, you're not saying your love or care for them is done. You are simply finished supporting their unhealthy lifestyle. I coach families to tell their unwell family members, "We are doing more harm than good with what we have been doing. Our way has not been working. We want to give you the best chance to be successful. We will always love you and will be here waiting when you are ready to get help and start working on a healthier lifestyle."

Equally important, the best statement an untreated person can say—both to themselves and to their families—is "I am done." Not done with living or having hope but finished living a dead-end lifestyle and ready to give healthier living a chance. Many times, they will reach this conclusion when they are completely desperate and no longer have battery life or gas in the tank. At this point, they surrender and recognize they are powerless over their disease. Please remember, powerless does not mean they are weak, or that the disease is unbeatable. It simply means they acknowledge they can't manage it on their own and will need a support team to take on the fight.

The Take Home:

Telling your loved one "We are done" supporting their unhealthy lifestyle can be a powerful motivator. "I am done" can also be one of the most impactful statements your loved ones can say to demonstrate they're ready to accept help.

My recommended statements for families with a chronically struggling member whose unhealthy lifestyle they no longer want to support:

"We are doing more harm than good with what we have been doing. Our way has not been working. We want to give you the best chance to be successful. We will always love you and will be here waiting when you are ready to get help and start working on a healthier lifestyle."

Must Know #21: Know That Treatment Is a Big Part of the Recovery Process—but Not the Only Part

What the Disease May Tell You

All Miranda needs is a few weeks in treatment, and she will be cured.

I'm sure once Quinton gets several weeks sober under his belt, alcohol won't be an issue anymore.

Madelyn's bipolar disorder merely needs a medication adjustment and some coping skills. Then, she won't have anything else to be concerned about.

Why important:

Family members sometimes think the recovery process is over once treatment ends. This "all done" mindset increases chances for reoccurring struggles.

Hopefully, you are now at the point when things are starting to come together. All of the strategies are working, and your affected family members have decided to get help. The family has also done the necessary legwork and found an appropriate treatment center. You are somewhat relieved but still fearful, as the situation can change directions at a moment's notice. But you've held strong to your boundaries and may even start to feel a little more hopeful.

I will talk in depth about the treatment process and long-term recovery in Chapters 7 and 9. I will explain what treatment entails and what the long-term recovery process may look like.

It's important to note that formal treatment (e.g., residential treatment program, intensive outpatient program with sober living, therapy with group home residence, etc.) is one of the most critical parts of the recovery journey, but only one part. In Chapter 7, I'll discuss the first thirty to ninety days of treatment, and how the family support system plays a vital role in increasing the probability of your unwell family member's success—both during treatment and throughout the complete recovery process.

Another important message I communicate to family members during this first phase of the process is that the goal of treatment is not to cure anyone. In addition to the more obvious aspects of treatment (e.g., mental and physical stabilization, the attainment of productive healthy coping skills, establishment of a healthy routine, improved family dynamics, etc.), the more overarching goal of treatment is to provide healthy choices and a preview of what a healthier life can look like. We can't force anyone into action or promise what the future holds, but we can help increase their probability of success by presenting better options.

To consider another angle, I know multiple cases of people who were forced into treatment (e.g., mandatory job requirement, boundaries set by family members, court-ordered treatment) and were *equally* as successful as people who were motivated to enter treatment voluntarily. I have witnessed this phenomenon countless times in my clinical work. During the first few weeks of treatment, when a person is so unhealthy that they are not thinking clearly, often they are in a psychotic state, under the influence of substances, or having uncontrolled emotional distress. As time goes on and stabilization occurs, they will often experience renewed insights about their lives, or have realizations about the people who care for them and feel a new desire to live; hence, they reach similar motivational levels as those who enter treatment on their own accord.

I spoke earlier about this drastic change in a person's desire to get better when I discussed the male in treatment who stated he wanted to kill his family members. After two weeks on medication and abstinence from methamphetamines, he was no longer manic and psychotic and had a strong desire to get better and finish treatment. Many times, family members have the false notion that their loved one can only improve if they are willing and have the desire to change, so they delay their interventive efforts. I coach family members to initiate the plan sooner rather than later. Don't wait for your loved one to "want treatment;" it is not a mandatory precursor to success.

Circling back to the topic of probability, the success of treatment and recovery is a numbers game in some ways. If a client is in treatment for one day, they increase their chances of making it to one week; if they are in treatment one week, they increase their chances of making it to one month; if they can remain in treatment one month, they increase their chances to stay on the path for six months; and if they can choose a healthier lifestyle for six months, they increase their chances for having one year of success. And, one year of treatment dramatically improves the likelihood of long-term recovery success. After a year, the process is not over and continued work towards healthier living is required. However, at this point the person has reached a lower level of acuity and has attained more automaticity and independence in their recovery program.

To remove any power struggles when clients first present to treatment groups, I let them know I will never argue over certain points: whether or not they are an addict, whether or not they can manage their substances, whether they need to take psychiatric medications or follow clinical recommendations, or whether or not they can still associate with the unhealthy people in their lives. In fact, I tell them that when discharged, they're more than welcome to re-engage in the lifestyle they lived prior to treatment, or to use their substance of choice. That lifestyle and substance are waiting right outside the door and will always be an option. But there is no guarantee their families will support that same lifestyle again. This is why it's critical for the family unit to maintain strong boundaries and clear messages about what they will advocate moving forward.

Earlier I stated that people will generally respond more favorably when they believe they have choices in a matter. Having the ability to choose provides a sense of empowerment and reduces the chance for resistance. Clients in treatment also have a choice. As adults, no one can tell them what they can and cannot do. However, what they need to realize is that others also have a choice about what they will be a part of and what they will not (a.k.a. boundary/limit setting). Family members may not be part of their unhealthy lifestyles moving forward, for the betterment of the complete family. The first thirty to ninety days can be the toughest period in early treatment, and I encourage clients to do whatever it takes to make this a one-time destination and not have to do it all over again. At the end of this conversation, I ask the group: "Who wants to do this treatment process all over again?" I always get a unified and resounding, "No!"

This idea of having a choice in the matter seems to resonate loud and clear. Ultimately, all decisions are theirs. I tell clients, "Either take advantage of the privilege (yes, treatment is a privilege—an opportunity not available to everyone) and maximize your success or face the same lifestyle you had before—one that is emotionally draining, physically taxing, dangerous, and filled with loss."

The Take Home:

The first phase of treatment is one of the most critical stages in the recovery process, which is why you have to do whatever it takes to get your struggling loved ones into this initial phase of getting help.

Must Know #22: Know the I.C.U (Intensive Care Unit) Can Also Mean I.H.C.U (I Have to Change Unit)

What the Disease May Tell You

What changes can happen this early in Jewel's treatment?
Jacklyn has been in treatment for three weeks and is still resentful.
That's a sure sign she will never get past the anger.

Jeremiah still dreams about drinking alcohol after two months in treatment. He is going to drink again for sure.

Why important:

Families need to realize that getting their struggling family members into the first phase of treatment is the hardest and the most difficult part of the process. Many times, families allow loved ones to abandon treatment at this juncture, causing the process to repeat all over again.

As you will see in Chapter 7, I refer to the first thirty to ninety days of treatment as Phase 1 of the recovery process. I encourage families to think of their unwell family members in this stage as though they're in the Intensive Care Unit (ICU) of a hospital. If you have been yourself or know of someone who has been admitted to the ICU, you know the circumstances are critical in nature, and immediate stabilization is the main goal. Some of the reasons a person may be admitted to the ICU are a stroke, injuries from a bad vehicle accident, substance overdose, heart attack, respiratory failure, etc. These dire situations are life or death cases.

This critical early treatment phase is similar to the ICU because in many ways, your untreated family members are in a life-or-death scenario. People enter treatment because the situations leading up to that point were quite bad, with a likelihood of deleterious consequences. I've had clients start treatment forty-eight hours after a suicide attempt, a few days after a drug overdose, or while experiencing active hallucinations due to ongoing, untreated psychiatric conditions.

Of course, the ICU in the hospital is very different in terms of the physical incapacities of patients in these units (e.g., in a coma, requiring intubation, in critical condition, etc.), but the idea of the heightened acuity of the person struggling to live is similar to how clients present in the first phase of treatment. Also, similar to the ICU, if patients do not receive immediate help, the outcomes can be life-changing or life-threatening.

I can't say what goes through the mind of someone in the ICU, but I know what goes through my mind at points of desperation. I can only imagine they are in a similar mental place. Perhaps they make resolutions or strike deals with their higher power. "I need to take better care of my body," I need to stop smoking," "I need to be more kind," "I need to manage my stress better," or "I need to appreciate my life more." When I reach a point of desperation, I think about the things in my life I should change to avoid the same predicament. Similarly, I hear clients in treatment repeat sentiments like, "I hate myself for getting to this point again," "I need to figure this out," "How do I get better?" or, "I really messed (euphemism for a more explicit word) things up this time." Therefore, the ICU can also be an *I Have to Change Unit* (I.H.C.U). Sometimes, this deep point of reflection can serve as an impetus for change, as they reach a point in their lives where "I'm done!" becomes a reality.

The Take Home:

Doing whatever it takes to get your loved ones into the first phase of treatment (ICU) is critical. This can be the point when they realize the need to change. "I'm done!" (I no longer want to live this unhealthy life and need to make a change) can be the most powerful two words your loved ones can utter during this phase of treatment.

Must Know #23: Know to Switch off the Repeat Cycle in Treatment and Don't Give in to P.A.W.S

What the Disease May Tell You

Although this is Felix's fifth time in treatment, maybe he will finally get it. It's okay to bail him out of jail.
Listen to Karl. That treatment center is not a good fit. The staff aren't attending to his needs promptly, the food is not tasty, and he can't relate to anyone because he is mentally stronger. Let him come home and find another treatment center.

> **Why important:**
>
> Families don't realize that, many times, they repeat the same patterns of behaviors, which allow their untreated family members to engage in an unhealthy lifestyle.

As you recall, I have provided several cases to illustrate how important the family system can be during the recovery process, particularly with healthy boundary setting. By contrast, you have also read about cases when families prolonged the struggle through enabling in the pre-treatment stage. Remember, why do people continue to engage in the same pattern of unhealthy living? *"Because they can!"* Switching off the merry-go-round mode (e.g., stop co-signing or agreeing to the unhealthy narrative) is essential. As you know, the disease can continue for a lifetime when the repeat button is pressed. It has no qualms about becoming a perpetual carousel ride, as long as there are willing participants.

If you've limited options and stayed firm, hopefully by now, everything is progressing according to plan, and your family members have entered the first phase of treatment. And yet, maybe you're fearful about how to avoid making this cycle, in and out of treatment, a chronic pattern. Some of the reasons families stay stuck in the repeat cycle are guilt, fear, sadness, and lack of faith in the treatment process. It is important to note, there are a few situations when a client will prematurely discharge, Against Clinical Advice (ACA) or Against Medical Advice (AMA), while in the treatment process: if the client and/or family believe a treatment center is egregious or negligent (e.g., below standard of care and putting person at heightened risk) or if client and/or family determine their struggling family member has a medical condition requiring a higher level of care (e.g., unmanaged diabetes, debilitating pain, dangerous heart condition, etc.). Unfortunately, early departures from treatment can most often be attributed to the manipulation aspect of the disease (I discuss more about manipulation in Chapter 5), as reasons are fabricated or feigned by the client in order to coerce family members to cosign their release. Certainly, a treatment center may truly be negligent and unsafe for a loved one, which is why due diligence is critical when conducting research, or a client may authentically have a medical issue that needs to be treated first. In my experience, more often than not, leaving treatment early is due to a client's desire to continue with the unhealthy lifestyle, or they are not ready to accept help. On the other hand, some examples of instances where a treatment team may initiate a premature discharge due to medical considerations are when your loved one needs a higher level of care (e.g., requiring surgery, organ failure, mental health issue are too acute for the level of care provided at the treatment facility or your loved one poses a threat to peers and staff members (e.g., verbal or physical threats).

Remember, the first thirty to ninety days are the toughest in the early treatment phase. An important concept to mention, one that is pervasive in the early phase of treatment, is Post-Acute Withdrawal Syndrome (PAWS). This is something your loved one may experience when they no longer have access to the malfunctioning life preserver (e.g., unhealthy coping tools). They want to hang on to this life preserver (because it works!) and they worry about how they will stay afloat without it. If you recall, this defective life preserver can be a substance of abuse, unhealthy thought patterns, dysfunctional behaviors, toxic people, dangerous places, or precarious situations.

PAWS involves all of the changes unwell people undergo when they are forced to give up their life preserver. These changes can be cognitive (e.g., attention span, memory, information processing), emotional/mental (e.g., anger, depression, resentment, anxiety, insomnia, suicidality, brief euphoria), physical (e.g., pain, heightened senses), and social (e.g., isolation, inferiority around others, social anxiety). The early phase of treatment is when PAWS (especially in the first thirty to ninety days) is most prominent, physical pain is greatest, and emotional discomfort and stress are most intense. Body and mind go through a major transition that will naturally cause a great deal of internal imbalance. Because of this, leaving treatment is common in the first thirty to ninety days, and families need to do whatever it takes to keep their loved one in care during this vulnerable window of the process. Remember, PAWS and other discomforts people in early recovery endure do get better over time, as the mind and body begin to heal and create a new life preserver more conducive to healthier living (e.g., therapy, mindfulness techniques, exercise, support groups, healthier diet, adequate sleep, proper medications, etc.).

The presentation and duration of PAWS vary across people. Some people experience it more intensely and for longer durations. Factors such as genetics, type of substances abused, the amount and duration of a substance's use, psychiatric diagnoses, individual adaptability, and ability to attain new protective factors (e.g., healthy coping tools) all may contribute to how your loved ones navigate through PAWS. Moreover, PAWS can last anywhere from a few weeks to two years. As long as a client is in treatment and abiding by all clinical recommendations, the symptoms of PAWS gradually wane over time. There can be occasional spikes (e.g., anxiety, memory lapses, social anxiety, depression, etc.) during this time period, but the intensity of these symptoms greatly lessens throughout the recovery process. PAWS is a natural consequence during the early phases of treatment and is not a valid reason to leave treatment prematurely. The symptoms will likely lessen as your recovering family members get healthier each day they stay committed to the treatment and recovery process.

The Take Home:

Stop feeding into the repeat cycle of the disease during the treatment process. The disease will take you on a never-ending, dead-end ride with high mental, emotional, and financial costs. Also, don't give in to PAWS! It's the natural aftermath of the disease's residual effects but gets better over time.

Must Know #24: Know About Relapse and Lapse—Siblings but Not Twins

What the Disease May Tell You

Ann relapsed on alcohol after treatment. This was all a waste of time and money!

Tyrese cut on himself again after six months of intense treatment. How could you think he is going to get past his PTSD?

> **Why important:**
>
> Family members need to realize that setbacks are likely to happen during the treatment and recovery process and should not be viewed as failures but rather as "data points" providing a great opportunity for growth and learning.

The first stage of treatment is now completed, and your recovering family members are on a path to continued healing. This period of time could be a few days, a couple of weeks, several months, or even a number of years. This brings me to an important point regarding the idea of a relapse or a lapse, post-treatment. The relapse and lapse notions are historically based around substance abuse (e.g., alcohol, heroin, painkillers, methamphetamines, etc.). This is a concept many educators on addiction and treatment specialists discuss with families and clients. Please note that these two concepts will be further discussed below, but for reference, a relapse is generally a major fall while a lapse is a slip. The likelihood your unwell family members may relapse or lapse on a substance, even after treatment, is high during the recovery journey. There are people who never relapse or lapse, and this path *is* very possible to achieve. However, it's important for family members and clients to realize relapsing or lapsing is not atypical. Even if it occurs, how quickly someone gets back on track is critical to their ability to rebound back towards their recovery path.

I prefer to speak on a relatable level in order to help everyone understand and empathize with the struggles family members may be enduring. For instance, I mentioned earlier we all have our own version of a disease (an entity causing impairment), and form of recovery (plans for healthier living and strategies to manage our own diseases). Please note, common attributes that are present in a strong recovery program will be further discussed in Chapters 5, 6, 7, and 9. I believe we are all vulnerable to relapses and lapses as well.

In this context, I define a relapse as any thoughts or behaviors we engage in after trying to lessen or eliminate them. People tend to think of a relapse in relation to alcohol or substances. However, relapse is broader than that. For instance, if a person's goal is to lessen work hours to devote more time to his kids, and he finds himself working eighty hours a week for a month, he had a relapse. If a manager wants to eliminate angry, blameful outbursts at her team members and finds herself yelling incessantly at her staff for several days, she had a relapse.

Furthermore, I extend the concept of relapse to include mental health conditions as well. For example, if a young female wants to lessen her manic episodes, and she finds herself in mania due to not managing her sleep, she had a relapse. A middle-aged male who has been working on avoiding depressive episodes but stops taking his anti-depressants may reach a point of relapse. If a young adult has been managing his delusional thoughts with a marriage and family therapist but decides to end therapy pre-maturely and begins experiencing paranoid delusions, he had a relapse.

I believe there is an inverse relationship (as one goes up, the other goes down) between the strength of one's recovery program and the likelihood of lapse or relapse. At the very least, a strong recovery program will have high levels of structure, routine, and accountability in place (weaker potential for relapse or lapse), while a weaker recovery program will have lower levels of structure, routine, and accountability (stronger potential for relapse or lapse). I will talk more about structure, routine, and accountability and what that may look like in Chapter 7.

Relapses are chronic, deep slides that are very difficult to recover from, especially with a weaker recovery program in place. Some examples of relapse behaviors can be when struggling loved ones repeatedly end up in the hospital for untreated mental health crises, or in and out of jail due to domestic abuse charges due to unresolved anger. A relapse could be indicated when someone can't maintain a steady, long-term abstinence from substances as a result of repressed child abuse, or they keep getting triggered into manic or depressive episodes or demonstrating other heightened symptoms due to not taking medications as prescribed. Recovering from a relapse is an arduous process, and it's difficult for someone to pull themselves out on their own volition. In worst case scenarios, people may suffer severe consequences when no support system is in place to help them get back on track.

On the other hand, a lapse is more of a brief slip back into unhealthy habits and is much easier to recover from when a strong recovery program is in place. Some examples of lapse behaviors can be a person who had maintained a few years of sobriety and reverted to using alcohol to cope with a sudden job loss but finding a healthy path back in a matter of days after connecting with a sobriety coach; someone with managed bipolar disorder suffering a manic episode after a distressing life event but seeking help from his treatment team and reaching re-stabilization; or, a female who had recovered from self-harm behaviors cutting on herself after a family member passes away, but working through the event with her therapist to stop subsequent cutting actions. People who have a lapse are better able to pull themselves out when there is structure, routine, and a support system holding them accountable and facilitating their progress back to healthier living.

Below are two figures to help explain the difference between a relapse and lapse. The figures I use to illustrate this difference are electrocardiograms (EKGs—a measure for electrical signals in the heart).

These images repeatedly flash in my mind when trying to help families visually understand the difference between a relapse and lapse.

Figure 3 represents the trajectory of a relapse. Remember, a weaker recovery program has an inverse relationship with relapse (the weaker the recovery program, the stronger the likelihood of relapse). The higher part of the EKG represents a person's baseline level of functioning, and the deep dips indicate relapses.

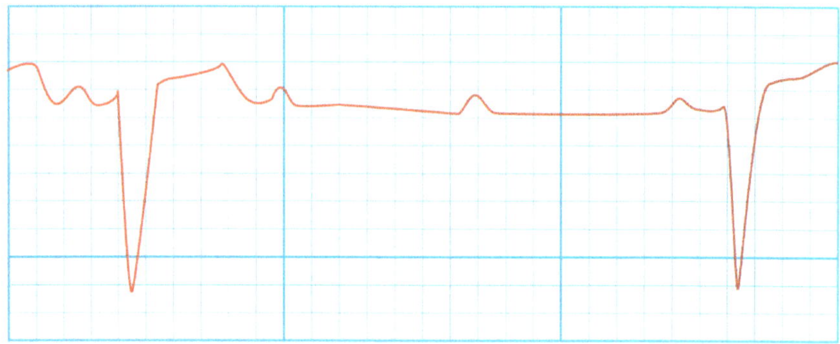

Figure 3. Graphic Illustration of a Relapse

Please refer to the above figure as I describe the following case to help you visualize the trajectory of relapses.

Gerald was a male in his twenties. He struggled with bipolar disorder and daily marijuana abuse, and he smoked wax (highly concentrated form of THC in the form of a yellow, waxy substance) four to five times a week. Also, he drank hard liquor heavily on the weekends. He did not have a therapist but saw his psychiatrist erratically, every six months or so. He was prescribed medications for his bipolar disorder but rarely took them, claiming they made him feel lethargic and lose creativity. In essence, he had a weaker recovery program.

Every three weeks or so, due to chronic substance use and not taking his prescribed medications, he would dip into a depressive episode. Without structure, routine, and a support network to hold him accountable, Gerald struggled each time to reach his baseline. He had no regimen or plan to get back on track. In order to manage his severe, depressive episodes, he turned to substances and ended up at the bottom for a long time. Several times, Gerald was hospitalized for hypomania and psychotic breaks, drug overdoses, or suicide attempts. He had stints in jail, due to DUIs or other law-breaking activities. Other times, he was homeless when he had overstayed his welcome with friends and relatives.

Eventually, Gerald was able to get back to his baseline, but it was a rough crawl and a steep, tiresome climb doing it all on his own. Without a recovery program in place, he would lay low for a little while, trying with sheer willpower to limit his substance use. Then a stressor would hit, and he would dip again. The cycle repeated for years, until he reached a level of desperation and asked for help. As you recall, willpower is important in recovery but only one of many attributes needed to be successful. As I noted earlier, sheer willpower is often referred to as "white knuckling" it, hanging on for dear life. In reality, people can only hang for so long before they fall. They need fellowship and a team to help them get through the struggles and keep them from falling again.

Figure 4 below represents how I envision the trajectory of a lapse. Remember, a stronger recovery program has an inverse relationship with relapses (the stronger the recovery program, the less likelihood of relapses and lapses). Moreover, a stronger recovery program increases the likelihood of eliminating lapses altogether. But lapses are usually infrequent and occur when a strong recovery program is in place because the person has a built-in plan (e.g., support system, healthy coping skills, accountability) to get back on a healthy path. The straighter lines of the EKG represent a person's baseline level of functioning, and the small dips indicate lapses.

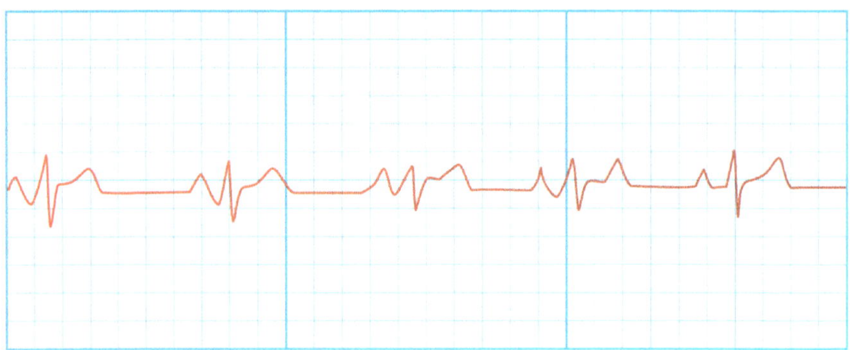

Figure 4. Graphic Illustration of a Lapse

Again, please refer to the above figure as I describe this following case to help you visualize the trajectory of lapses. Please note, though lapses are potential events in the post-treatment phase, I do not want to convey that experiencing them is an expected norm. I am not giving clients or families *permission* to lapse. Ideally, the goal is for loved ones never to relapse or lapse moving forward, due to the inherent dangers with any falls or slips in recovery.

Carly was a female in her late twenties who struggled with alcohol and heroin, depression, and past suicidality. She finished residential treatment, joined intensive outpatient groups, saw her therapist and psychiatrist regularly, attended substance support meetings daily, and worked sobriety steps with her sponsor. She also took her medications as prescribed. Carly had a strong family support system, a part-time job, and she attended college classes. In essence, she had a stronger recovery program.

After eighteen months into her recovery, Carly lost a dear friend to a drug overdose. She was in a highly distressed state and to cope with her sadness, she lapsed with a bottle of wine. Knowing what she had done and not wanting to spiral further, she immediately called her sponsor and therapist and came clean to her family about what she had done. She also revealed her lapse to the peers in her intensive outpatient group. Carly immediately got back on track due to the accountability she had in place and a strong support system of family, peers, and clinicians to help direct her back to the recovery path. She also had ample amounts of healthy coping skills (healthy life preserver) she had attained in treatment to manage her emotional distress. Without this recovery program, Carly most likely would have found herself back in relapse mode, shooting heroin, drinking excessive amounts of alcohol, and most likely, making another suicide attempt.

So, what does a relapse or lapse mean for the recovery process? Family members have called me, absolutely distraught when their loved ones have lapsed after completing residential treatment, even if they were able to get back on track due to a strong recovery program. They'll say, "This was all a waste of time," or, "What was the use?" After validating their feelings of anger, disappointment, and sadness, my question to family members is, "Prior to treatment, what has been the outcome of a relapse?" I would hear answers such as, "She would have eventually attempted suicide," "He would have ended up in the psychiatric unit after a psychotic break," or, "She would have gone on a long alcohol bender." I encourage the families to reflect about how far their loved ones have come along since treatment, and how they are breaking major patterns by not spiraling back down those dark paths. Often, family members let out a sigh of relief as they think it through, grateful their loved one is back on a road to recovery and not experiencing those previous outcomes.

Remember what author James Clear said about *data points*. Setbacks, adversity, or failures need to be viewed as information from which to grow. Lapses are the same. The goal is for your recovering family members to learn from lapses and further strengthen their recovery programs. Learning from past mistakes also significantly prevents lapses from turning into relapses. Your family members need to know they have the capabilities to get better and fight the disease, if they make the conscious choice to do so. As motivational speaker Eric Thomas said, "Every human has what it takes to get past what they are going through, if they decide to."

After treatment, if loved ones have a relapse, most likely they never created a strong enough recovery program to begin with, weren't ready to change their old lifestyle, their family members did not maintain firm boundaries and engaged in old family patterns, or they gravitated back to unhealthy people, triggering places, old, dysfunctional thinking patterns, or troublesome situations from the past.

The Take Home:

Know that a lapse is very likely during the early recovery process and a probable but not absolute trajectory of the journey. Rather than a failure, it can be an opportunity for greater growth. A revision to the recovery program may be essential to not only prevent relapses but also lessen the chances of lapses.

Must Know #25: Know About Validation—The Best Medicine for Communication

What the Disease May Tell You

Janice has a psychotic disorder, so she doesn't know what she wants or needs!

Tristan has no idea how he feels. He is too high all the time.

Obviously, Tabatha has no idea what she is talking about and is seeking attention with her crying bouts.

Why important:

Sometimes families overlook how communication patterns can mean the difference between connecting and not connecting with their unwell family members. When families are not connecting, it can cause further distancing and polarization.

Earlier, I mentioned the continuing education seminar that was life-changing for me as a clinician. There, I learned one of the most invaluable tools integral to my practice (i.e., the one-time, 7.5-minute introduction with a client for the purpose of not allowing them to repeat their unhealthy narrative in each meeting without making healthy changes). The other groundbreaking tool I took home that is still part of my clinical arsenal today is validation.

Validation

Validation is the process of accepting someone's truth. This acceptance doesn't mean you have to believe or agree with the person's truth, it simply means you acknowledge it, and have reached a level of acceptance and understanding to interact more effectively. Validation is as close as you can get to empathy (truly acknowledging and understanding another person's experience). In fact, I view validation as an essential precursor to empathy. This approach is similar to the idea of improving cultural competencies. When enhancing our cultural understanding, we are asked to try to immerse ourselves in the other person's culture to understand and interact better.

We've heard various analogies of this concept. "Put yourself in their shoes," "Understand where they're coming from," or "Look at it from their perspective." All of these speak to validation, a way to see and hear the other person. It's not simply recognizing and listening to a person, but truly grasping the essence of where the person is emotionally, mentally, and physically. I like to use the metaphor of trading glasses and looking, understanding, and experiencing the other person's worldview from their lenses.

Invalidation

Conversely, the antithesis of validation is invalidation. This process is literally the near opposite of what validation entails. Invalidation involves not acknowledging or rejecting someone's truth as well as not seeing or hearing what that person is trying to communicate. Invalidation results when a person can't or won't try on the other person's glasses to try to understand their worldview.

Perhaps you have experienced both validation and invalidation and know what each feels like. Let's say you are on the phone with a customer service representative, trying to return a pricey item you bought online that has a ten-day return policy. You had a family crisis and didn't have access to the internet, and now it's one day past the refund date. The customer service representative refuses to budge, reminding you that the due date to get your money back is "set in stone." The audacious representative even squeezes in the remark that you should have paid closer attention to the date—all responses in line with invalidation.

You try to keep your cool, tapping into every self-soothing technique imaginable but reaching a level of frustration and anger. Before blurting out an expletive you may regret, you begrudgingly but politely ask for the manager. When the manager gets on the call, he says, "I understand there is an issue with a return past the due date. I am so sorry to hear about your family crisis and hope all is okay. I am sorry to hear of your frustrations with the return process. What I am hearing you say is that due to the family crisis, returning the item was impossible before the due date. Let's see what we can do to make this better for you." Even as I type out this (somewhat) fictional scenario, I felt the emotions of both invalidation and validation flow through me. You may not get a dime back but will feel better as the manager saw, heard, and listened to you.

Tools for Validation

Two of the most effective ways to validate someone are: 1) Identifying an emotion ("You sound hurt," "That must be disheartening," "I can feel how lonely you must be)," and 2) Rephrasing ("What I am hearing you say is…" "What you are telling me is…" "Based on what you are explaining to me is that…)" Both tactics convey to the person that you are tracking their words and actively trying to grasp what they are trying to communicate.

The manager did both eloquently, by identifying your emotions and rephrasing what you were trying to explain. Plus, it made the manager's job easier and created a win-win situation for everyone involved when validation took place.

It is also worth noting, there are hundreds of words to describe feelings. But people often stick to the most common ones when describing their emotions or reflecting to someone of how they may be feeling (happy, mad, sad, and frustrated). These words are not inherently wrong but sometimes do not capture the true essence of how a person may be feeling. Words such as rejected, lonely, abandoned, minimized, hopeful, heard, and cheerful may further validate someone and convey that you are grasping what they are going through. By the way, as a clinician, I ask clients to come up with additional words when they use angry, mad, and frustrated to describe their feelings, as these can be more culturally accepted but can be secondary to a more sensitive emotion such as feeling betrayed, ashamed, and vulnerable. A simple internet search of "feeling words" will yield many lists and charts of emotions. Increasing one's feeling vocabulary is not only great for improving your Emotional IQ (the ability to understand, utilize, and manage one's emotions that can then be used for activities such as empathizing with others, problem solving, or self-soothing) but also effective for strengthening your validation skills.

I promise, if you do these two simple validation techniques in any of your relationships (e.g., parent to child, spouse to spouse, romantic partner to romantic partner, friend to friend, medical provider to a patient, staff member to customer, business partner to business partner, boss to employee, co-worker to co-worker, etc.), I guarantee you will dramatically increase your chances of getting past the first base of communication—the place where most communication ends because other perspectives are not seen, heard, or accepted. First base is where blaming, name-calling, abandonment of discussion, and verbal warfare take place because of invalidation. Try validation; you will witness for yourself how integral it is in better communication with others and how reaching a consensus— the ultimate goal in conflict resolution—becomes much easier.

Case examples with validation

Here are three case examples to further illustrate how important validation can be. First, a single mother came to see me due to a contentious relationship with her thirteen-year-old daughter. The girl repeatedly said things like, "You don't understand me," You don't get my generation," and, "You never listen to me." The mother said she had tried everything to support her daughter and couldn't understand why she felt so disconnected. I asked her to provide an actual example of a challenging situation that had occurred to help me better understand what may be going on between them. She mentioned that recently, her daughter had come home from school melancholy and tearful, saying she hated everyone and never wanted to go back. Upon further examination, the mother learned that two of the girl's best friends had unfriended her on social media because of rumors that she was talking behind their backs. The daughter insisted she hadn't. The nurturing and protective mother immediately chimed in, "You don't need them. That is totally their loss. There are so many other people out there who will treat you nicely. Those aren't real friends and need to get rid of them. In my days, we didn't have social media, so I don't get it."

The daughter retreated quietly back to her room, while the mother thought her points were well-taken, and she had hit a home run. She didn't realize that she wasn't hearing her daughter, validating her, or trying to understand her truth. Although she was coming from a loving, parental place, she wasn't putting on her daughter's glasses. I suggested she could have said something like, "I am so sorry to hear that happened to you. You sound very hurt that your two friends removed you from their social network. I am also hearing that you thought they were your close friends, but they didn't give you the benefit of the doubt. Does that sound right? How can I best support you?" The mother understood the reasoning behind the validation approach and tried it the next time an issue arose. She reported a much better response, and she and her daughter had an intimate dialogue as a result.

A second example came about in a family group in treatment for a female in her late twenties who struggled with substance-induced psychosis. During a session, the daughter said she and her father hadn't gotten along for years, due to his lack of understanding about her spiritual journey and the way he pressed his religious beliefs on her. The daughter wanted to get in touch with her spirituality and find her own journey to a higher power. In our family group, I facilitated an exercise on validation skills. I asked the daughter and father to identify each other's emotions and rephrase what they believe the other was saying. The daughter said she felt trapped and judged by her father for not adopting the family's religious beliefs. The father said he had always been open to her spiritual journey but wondered how she could ever be certain about her beliefs when she was in psychotic episodes. He didn't want her spiritual journey to be influenced by mild-altering substances.

The daughter immediately had an "aha" moment and understood the truth in her father's reasoning. She apologized for her past actions and agreed she couldn't arrive at a true belief system as long as she wasn't sober. Both the father and daughter went from years of invalidation to validation in a matter of five minutes, simply by identifying each other's emotions, rephrasing what the other was saying, and arriving at a consensus (i.e., support her spiritual beliefs as long as she came to her beliefs in sobriety).

The last example shows that even with someone in an active psychotic state, validation is an effective tool for communication. I was working with a middle-aged male who presented with a psychotic disorder (e.g., auditory and visual hallucinations) and had over twenty years of abstinence from any mind-altering substances. During our preliminary intake session while gathering background information, he stated that his ex-wife had been living upstairs with her boyfriend for the past few years. He said she would sometimes yell expletives, and he believed these utterances were directed at him. He also noted that she still had a key to the apartment they had lived in together. Nothing seemed out of the ordinary, as I have worked with divorced couples who continued to live together for financial reasons and even had new, romantic partners visit the residence. It wasn't until our third session together, he told me he believed his ex-wife was trying to steal the cat crate in his apartment, which was causing him a great deal of stress. I asked how she was trying to steal it. He calmly said that she came through an opening in the ceiling of his closet, which led to the attic. He looked at me and asked if I thought he was crazy. I said, "I don't think you're crazy. I believe something is causing you a great deal of stress, and I want to help lower your stress." As you can imagine, his question most likely was a result of many people giving him a "You're kidding me" look and challenging his belief system. I didn't agree or necessarily believe that his ex-wife was upstairs, but I did validate his truth.

It is important to note, he was situated on the top floor of the apartment building, with no living space or attic above. His ex-wife had not been in contact with him for over ten years, and, more surprisingly, according to his son, she hadn't lived in the same state for many years. Further, my client told me that the apartment manager, a maintenance worker, and even the police had informed him there was only roof space above his apartment unit. In his eyes, everyone was invalidating him and not understanding his viewpoint. Of course, these people were simply reporting the facts. I learned that he had recently stopped taking his antipsychotic medications. From a clinical standpoint, my goal was to get him back on his medication regimen.

I told him if he started taking his medication, his stress levels would decrease and his experiences with his ex-wife wouldn't bother him as much. He agreed and got back on his medication. Unsurprisingly, he didn't have many complaints about his ex-wife after that.

Transitional words and validation/invalidation

One last recommendation for effective communication and validation is by omitting transitional words as much as possible, especially when trying to work towards resolution. This type of word can act as barriers to effective resolution, specifically ones that are used for contrast. For those who need a quick English 101 refresher, transitional words (aka "conjunctive adverbs") in the English language are words that link sentences or paragraphs together. They are very important in writing, adding flow and cohesiveness for the writer and reader. Different types of transitional words have various functions. The one type of transitional words I strongly discourage in communications intended for validation and working on resolutions are contrast ones (e.g., "but," "however," "on the other hand"). These words provide contrary meaning, and what they essentially do in heated exchanges, verbal disagreements, or when trying to resolve an issue, is create more distance and disconnect between the parties involved.

We have all been there, in an emotional exchange with someone who uses kind words and compliments up front, followed by a contrast transitional word. Instantly, we lose sight of the nice things and wait in distress for what's to follow. We get into a defensive mode because what comes next is usually something negative. In other words, we feel the compliments were a way to soften the coming blow. My visualization of this concept is a bright, sparkling train front engine being followed by a series of train cars all on fire.

As an example, let's say a husband and wife are having an argument about the husband's decision-making on his spending. The wife, trying to come from a good place, says, "I think you have a great head on your shoulders and are very smart with so many decisions in your life, **BUT** you tend to not pay attention to your budget." Then it's on, verbal warfare takes place on both ends, verbal bullets start flying, blame follows, and they find themselves talking about a comment made at Thanksgiving dinner fifteen years ago, entirely unrelated to spending.

A similar situation to exemplify this idea is an employer providing feedback to an employee. The nervous employee is called into the boss's office and the boss says, "You are a good team member and I always appreciate your hard work; **HOWEVER,** your performance over the past few weeks is not meeting standards." Once the employee hears "however," his heart starts palpitating and his blood pressure rises as the words "good team member" and "hard work" are a long gone, a distant memory. What's even worse, a momentary pause after the transitional word, "however," (by the way, the longer the pause, the worse it is), makes it more distressful for the recipient. More often than not, what follows this type of transitional word, preceded by a favorable statement, is not pleasant.

The amazing thing is that by simply leaving out the contrast transition word, you can still communicate the point, while greatly minimizing the chances for a negative reaction, defensiveness, or resistance.

In the two above examples, simply leaving out the transitional words (and maybe, making a few, minor revisions to the statement) can make a world of difference and open the possibility of getting to the second base of resolution (restating the problem). Please note, in my model of conflict resolution, second base (restating the problem of focus and expressing the reasons for change), third base (each party stating their requests) and home base (arriving at a consensus whereby a decision is made that satisfies each party to some extent) are the remaining steps in the process once moving past first base is achieved. Remember, most people get stuck on first base due to invalidation. In the example of the husband and wife, she could say, "I think you have a great head on your shoulders and are very smart with many decisions in your life. I would appreciate it if you could pay closer attention to your budget." You can feel the difference simply by omitting "**BUT**" and adding a word or two to make the statement more favorable. For the workplace example, the boss could have said, "You are a good team member and I always appreciate your hard work. Let's explore your performance over the past few weeks, as it is not meeting current standards." Again, what a world of difference by leaving out the word "**HOWEVER**," especially if the goal is to get your point across effectively, keep the person engaged, and reach a resolution.

Trust me, if you try this in all areas of your life, you will see the difference it makes. Use the same approach with your unwell family members. They are on edge to begin with, possibly impaired emotionally and cognitively, and resistant to any criticism. This approach can help avoid a further disconnect and give you more opportunities to plant emotional seeds and get your point across.

To summarize, putting yourself in someone else's shoes or fully seeing the world through their lens is a critical way to create intimate connections. I help clients in treatment realize and validate their families' emotions (e.g., desperation, fear, love, care), to understand why they did what they did to help. Once clients start to get healthy, the reasons their families acted in such a manner (e.g., calling the police, putting them in treatment, breaking promises as a desperate way to get a loved one help)

become more valid and clear. I also work with families in treatment to validate what their struggling family members in recovery may be going through (e.g., fear, panic, anxiety, sadness, shame, regret, guilt), to help them empathize with the loved one's past struggles and what they are enduring in the early phases of treatment. Making simple tweaks in our communications, such as removing contrast transitional words, can make a world of difference. If clients and families can diligently work at understanding each other's worldview and improving interpersonal skills, the building blocks for healthier communications can emerge.

The Take Home:

Validation is one of the most important tools in communication. It's also a major element in establishing relationships with your loved ones and a critical ingredient in assertive love.

A good example of statements you can use to convey care and support yet set boundaries while eliminating a contrasting transitional word (e.g., but, however) are:

"We love you and want to be here for you. We cannot support your unhealthy lifestyle any longer. When you are ready to accept help and decide to get on a healthy path, we will be here waiting and supporting you every way we can."

There they are, the 25 most essential pieces of knowledge I believe provide the ammunition to fight the disease as well as establish a critical, instrumental base when creating a robust plan for getting your loved ones help and on a path to long-term healthiness. This knowledge is based on thematic questions, concerns, and challenges families and unwell loved ones face continually in my clinical work. Please refer back to these Must Knows as needed for a reminder, refresher, or to educate others about the recovery process.

Chapter 5

Treating the Disease

This chapter will further discuss the disease and the 80-20 model I developed to help family members understand the sole purpose behind my strategies—shutting down one of the most problematic attributes of the disease—manipulation. I will define my 80-20 model, tell you what it entails, and explain why it is important. Additionally, I will discuss the three factors that I believe compromise the disease's vaccine.

80-20 Model

Over the years in my work with clients presenting with a multitude of conditions, family members consistently discuss the manipulation aspect of the disease. Generally speaking, manipulation is the act of getting others to engage in behaviors they normally would avoid or prefer not to engage in. Some examples of manipulative tactics are lying, using anger, blaming, bullying, threatening, stonewalling, pretending to be naïve, playing victim, using sex, power, money, knowledge or people. It is important to reiterate, I am not taking accountability or responsibility from your struggling family members and pinning their challenges solely on the disease. My purpose is to identify the disease as a separate entity with weaknesses, so we can come up with a strategy to exploit and fight it. One way of exploiting its weaknesses is by strategizing against its manipulative aspects.

No matter the diagnosis, substance of abuse, or level of severity, manipulation is the most recurring challenge families face. When counseling countless families, I wondered what percentage certain aspects of the disease are accounted for in their family members' dysfunction. What I find is that there are two main distinctions when ascertaining the disease's dysfunction—the valid reasons and the manipulation aspect. In other words, there are legitimate reasons for their struggles (e.g., traumas, family dysfunction, medical conditions, psychiatric diagnoses, addictions, etc.), but the manipulative aspect of the disease prevents those struggling with mental health and addiction from doing the necessary work to get better. The manipulative side of the disease acts as a barrier to addressing the valid reasons because it wants the person to stay unwell and suffering. My best estimate of the breakdown between valid reasons and the manipulative aspect of the disease is eighty percent valid reasons and twenty percent manipulation. Manipulation is the disease's strongest line of defense, a protective layer of armor, or the moat that thwarts treatment from reaching and eventually disempowering it. Please see Figure 5 for a pictorial representation of my 80-20 disease model.

Whether families seek help in my family support group, private practice, or in treatment, the most important strategy is to shut down the manipulative components of the disease. Unwell family members engage in unhealthy patterns of behavior and struggle to make headway with their conditions because of the disease's manipulation, which acts as a blockage from addressing these deeply entrenched issues.

Some more examples of the valid reasons people struggle are chronic fears, unresolved resentments, childhood traumas, experience with bullying, sexual abuse, physical abuse, assaults, dysfunctional family dynamics, genetic conditions, medical issues, low self-worth, life-altering events, etc. All of these are important and critical issues to work through in recovery. But the path to healing needs to be created by shutting down the manipulative aspect of the disease—this is the most important step to laying that foundation.

For example, I met a female client in her thirties who had attempted treatment several times throughout her life but had left prematurely and relapsed on substances. Each time, she'd find herself back in a depressive episode. She had suffered past sexual trauma and the loss of a parent at a young age—two very tragic experiences causing severe impairment in her life. She abandoned treatment because she wasn't ready to work on her traumas, and her family allowed her to return home due to their overwhelming guilt. To further perpetuate the issues, her family members never asked her to take on responsibilities such as a job or school, as they were worried the stress involved in these two arenas would put her in a downward, emotional spiral. Essentially, they were underestimating her insight and awareness. Whenever family members encouraged her to get a job or seek help for her struggles, she would get angry, remind them of the traumas she had endured, and threaten to end her life.

If you recall, tactics to shut down the manipulative side of disease are discussed in Chapter 4, *Must Know #13: Know to Recognize the Hope in Desperation (Let Go of the Emotional Tug-of-War)*. In the above case, I recommended the family stop providing money to supply her substance use, limit places where she could sleep when she overstayed her welcome at other family members' homes, and cease paying for the gasoline in her car. I also reminded them to use assertive love and to continue planting emotional seeds (e.g., tell her she matters and is loved immensely). Shortly afterwards, the client reached a level of desperation and agreed to treatment. She realized she couldn't avoid dealing with her traumas forever and imagined a better life supported by a family who loves her. Not surprisingly, she attempted to leave treatment after a few days, but her family held firm to their boundaries. By not giving in to the manipulation tactics that had worked so well in the past, she started to engage in the long overdue, deep work on her past traumas.

Sometimes families share their own ideas of a percentage breakdown in relation to their untreated family members' dysfunction. One family told me, "Our son's issues are more like eighty percent manipulation and twenty percent valid reasons," while another shared, "My daughter's struggles are ninety-five percent manipulation and five percent valid." In these cases, I would assist with validation techniques, as their unwell family member's own self-assessment of their valid struggles may be much higher, especially when they are likely unaware of the manipulative aspects. The point is not about agreeing upon percentages but rather, recognizing there is a portion of your loved one's struggles—a manipulative side—that needs to be managed before they can work on the deep-rooted issues that are keeping them stuck in their unhealthy states.

Although it's optimal to shut down most—if not all—of the manipulative side of your loved one's disease, that may not always be possible. In many instances, residual aspects of the manipulative portion of the disease might continue to appear as artifacts in their actions (e.g., blaming, using anger, threatening, stonewalling, etc.). These residual traits will be part of their treatment and recovery journey as they may be hard-engrained habits, dysfunctional coping skills, and unconventional actions previously engaged to survive and cope. One of the major goals of treatment and recovery is to help them find other healthy habits to manage their lives more effectively and greatly minimize or eradicate these residual, unhealthy aspects at some point in the recovery process.

As I mentioned earlier, struggling loved ones use unhealthy coping skills as their life preserver "because it works." For this reason, these habits may still be a part of their unhealthy repertoire, especially in the early stages of the treatment process. In the pre-treatment phase, shutting down the twenty percent manipulation component is crucial, because it precludes them from getting any type of help.

Families need to acknowledge their power in the situation and realize that shutting down the manipulative side of the disease is a critical strategy in getting their untreated family members help. Approaches mentioned earlier in the book such as assertive love, setting loved ones up for desperation, sticking to the non-negotiables, limiting options, and planting emotional seeds are effective ways to destabilize the disease. We will discuss the plan in more detail in Chapter 8.

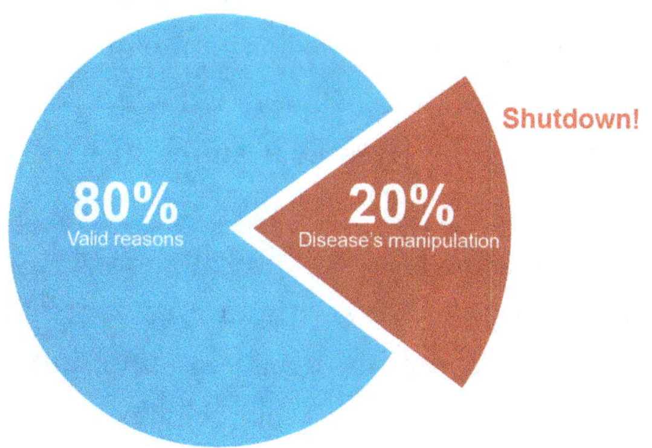

Figure 5. 80-20 Disease Model

Important Note:

Remember, in addition to the manipulative aspect of the disease, families can often underestimate their loved ones' insight and awareness (which can result from a manipulation tactic if they are playing a naïve or unaware role). This underestimation leads to enabling, guilt, and fear—powerful barriers to getting your loved ones working on the other eighty percent.

The disease vaccine (H2O)

This section will discuss attributes that distinguish people who are successful from those not successful in the treatment and recovery processes. These are the attributes I have found to be the most common in clients able to maintain long-term, healthy lifestyles. In fact, they are so prevalent, I refer to them as the disease's vaccine.

Before moving forward, it is worth noting how I define success in recovery from a mental health perspective. Success is when a person is moving consistently in the intended direction (e.g., continued sobriety, better managing depressive symptoms, acquiring healthy coping tools, etc.) and a lack of success is when a person is simply not moving towards their intended direction (e.g., multiple relapses, not consistently taking medications, constant exposure to unhealthy relationships, etc.). Many times, success is focused on the result or outcome, but the process involved in attaining that success is forgotten. For instance, a person solely focused on attaining one year of sobriety may view that outcome as the only marker of success. Instead, that person should view each day without a lapse or relapse and the strategies mastered to accomplish this goal as monumental progress. Motivational speaker Tony Robbins takes this notion a step further and states that *progress equals happiness.* This highlights the importance of appreciating process over outcome.

In the "Must Knows," I shared some of the critical knowledge and tactics for getting your family members help. By now, you should have foundational knowledge about how the disease manifests, increased awareness of your challenging family patterns, and a better understanding of your role in supporting your loved one's healthier lifestyle.

Now, we'll discuss the traits your struggling ones need to have during the recovery program to be successful and keep the disease at bay. In my work with hundreds of clients at individual and group levels, the same recurring themes emerge, separating those who stay sober from those who fall off the program, those who manage their diseases from those who stay untreated, and those who progress from those who remain stagnant or regress.

The three attributes I consistently witness in those successful in sobriety and/or managing their mental health are: <u>Honesty</u>, <u>Humility</u>, and <u>Openness to Direction</u> (H2O). Yes, H2O (water) is an essential element for survival and life, and it's essential in sobriety and managing mental illness. In fact, my H2O model is one the most powerful protective factors in managing the disease and an essential ingredient in the vaccine's formula. Let me explain H2O in more detail.

Honesty

I firmly believe the most important element for any type of change to occur, especially in the recovery process, is honesty. This means being honest with oneself and with others. If people are not completely honest, they are harboring secrets. These secrets will eventually turn into resentments, which I call unresolved anger. The metaphor I use when explaining resentments to families and clients is a pot of boiling oil. The oil boiling over the pot's edge, clearly visible, is anger. It is obvious, apparent, and usually easy to see (e.g., yelling at someone, road rage, punching a wall). When most of the hot oil is poured out, the remaining, residual oil at the bottom—not always visible but still seething hot—is resentment. I call resentments the "termites of our souls" or "acid of our infrastructure," as they slowly eat and rot away our healthy, inner vitalities. If you look at almost any type of treatment modality, therapeutic approach, religious teaching, sobriety program, meditative practice, or better health routine, working on letting go of resentments is at the core. Resentments can be destructive if not attended to, causing harmful outcomes such as long-term distress, a predisposition for heart disease, fractured relationships, and the stunting of emotional or spiritual growth.

Unlike anger, an emotion on the surface or worn on the proverbial sleeve, resentments are lurking in the background, sometimes forgotten until the perfect storm arises, or a retrieval cue prompts its memory. A case example of how resentments can be off the grid but still lurking was a male client who was in his mid-eighties. He was seeking ways to be happier in life after the loss of his wife several years before. He had done a great deal of work on grief and loss in his support group and was in the acceptance phase. Having moved on with his life, he was even open to new companionship if it were to happen.

Easy-going and mild-mannered, he was, overall, in a good place but needed guidance on how to feel more fulfilled in life and set new goals.

After a few sessions, I asked him one day about his career (he had been retired for thirty years). The happy-go-lucky gentleman quickly shifted to an uptight man with stiff body language. He told me at his last job before retirement, his departure had not gone how he had envisioned. Back then, they still used timecards to clock in and out. One day, as he went to the timeclock as he had been doing for ten years, a stickie note was on his card. It stated, "No more hours."

He looked at me, his eyes blazing. "That was the sendoff I got for a decade of hard work?" No one had informed him or given him an inkling he was going to be let go. He had been a contract worker, but he still couldn't imagine treating someone who had committed so much time to an organization in such a dismissive way.

There it was, resentment at its strongest, as observed in his flushed skin, angry tone of voice, tight lips, and tilted eyebrows. He said he hadn't talked about that event for nearly thirty years. Thinking it was long behind him, he was astonished by how raw it still felt. Before he could reach true fulfillment, he knew he had some grieving and resentments to work on. This was a classic example of how resentments can go unnoticed, brewing deep in the recesses to resurface under the perfect conditions.

I tell my clients in recovery or private practice that I can only help them with whatever they tell me. At the end of the day, if they're not honest or avoid discussing an uncomfortable issue, I say, "You have to look in the mirror at night and know it's just you and your disease. Once the session is over, I am off to the next appointment or client, and you are only inflicting harm on yourself by not working on getting better." Clients have avoided telling psychiatrists they are still hearing voices, so they won't get a higher dose of meds. To avoid worrying their families, some don't tell their therapist about strong desires to use their drug of choice. Others fail to inform staff they feel unsafe and have thoughts of cutting on themselves, to prevent adding more time to their treatment. I advise clients to "tell on yourselves" and be honest. The more up front they are, the better we can formulate a plan to help them and prevent symptoms from getting worse.

I also ask clients to be honest about *everything*! They can't pick and choose. When I ask clients in a group session, "If you are honest about one hundred secrets in treatment but refuse to talk about the one secret you never want to disclose, what is most likely going to take you out?" In unity, they agree it would be that one, hidden secret. This secret is usually avoided due to shame, regret, guilt, embarrassment, and fear of what may come about as a result of being honest. Naturally, in treatment, much of the focus is on the clients—those who have harmed them, traumas they endured, and losses they've suffered in life. But it would be remiss to ignore the mammoth elephant in the room. Clients need the space to consider and process the times they may have inflicted harm onto others (e.g., violence, physical abuse, verbal abuse, sexual abuse, other crimes, etc.). This type of secret, if not worked through, will continue to perpetuate guilt, shame, sadness, and regret. This is the reason I advise clients to "come clean ASAP" when they feel that harboring a secret is leading them down a path of unhealthiness. Swiss psychiatrist Carl Jung once said, "Whatever you resist persists."

In the case of circumstances in which people were harmed, or they harmed others, resentments are likely. What I have found is that resentments almost always point back at oneself, even when that person was the one victimized. I had a client who was physically beaten as a young, five-year-old child by her alcoholic mother. She was eventually taken away by Child Protective Services and for many years was resentful towards her mom for not being present in her life. Even at eighty years of age, she mostly resented herself for allowing it to happen, and for not protecting herself

Of course, we know a five-year-old doesn't have the means to fend for herself against a full-grown adult. Still, her resentment was directed inward. Resentment that turns to self-blame is quite common in my work, which is why I believe resolving resentments is critical to success.

Lastly, I tell clients being honest doesn't mean they have to open up to everyone or shout their secrets from the hilltops. But they do need to confide in at least one living person on this earth. It can be a pastor, priest, therapist, clinician, sponsor, life coach, etc. These are people who can view you through an objective lens, who are not afraid to give you honest feedback, and who aren't overly worried about the emotional side of the process. In other words, they can offer critical feedback unlike family members, who may worry about hurting feelings and be unable to offer unbiased reactions and feedback.

Clients have asked me, "What if I gave it to God?" "What if I told the Universe?" "How about if I spoke to Human Nature?" These are wonderful options, but there is something even more cathartic in the process if you can give your secrets to someone who can respond, support, and provide immediate validation. I strongly recommend clients consider being honest with at least one living person, due to the impact this process (e.g., validation, release from self-guilt, lessen resentments) can have on the path to healthiness.

By practicing honesty, your loved ones will not allow the disease to lurk in the shadows. Instead, it will be rendered vulnerable, as it is exposed and constantly talked about. The disease is most effective when it is being ignored or forgotten. Staying in honesty is the most important component of the H2O vaccine.

What a person with a <u>low</u> degree of honesty may sound like:

I don't need to talk about my (insert drug of choice) cravings because they will pass.

My mania is coming back, but I don't want to tell my psychiatrist because she will increase my dosage.

I have been cutting on myself due to my recent breakup. I need to keep it to myself because they will throw me back in the hospital.

I've been having thoughts about dying and even have a plan, but I usually stop having the thoughts once I drink a little.

What a person with a <u>high</u> degree of honesty may sound like:

I need to tell my therapist about someone I harmed while I was using alcohol.

My depression is getting much worse and need to call my psychiatrist as soon as possible.

I have strong desires to use meth but need to tell my sponsor about these desires.

Humility

According to Merriam-Webster Dictionary, *humility* is defined as "not proud" or not "showing superiority." This is another vital component of H2O. Humility in recovery means always respecting the capabilities of the disease and never believing you are superior. Once we start denying its power, that's when the disease gets back to work. I advise clients to always respect what they are up against; if they don't, they are harboring too much pride and displaying superiority. Please, don't confuse humility with a lack of confidence or sense of disempowerment. Having humility, in this case, means appreciating the capabilities of the entity challenging you (e.g., opponent, traumatic experience, medical condition, social circumstance, mental health disorder, addiction, etc.). I ask clients, "What happens if you disrespect the ocean (if you engage in water sports or activities), the mountains (if you are a skier or hiker), or the forest (if you are a camper or hiker)?" I always get the same response: "You get badly hurt or die!" The way to respect these entities is to prepare appropriately. Respect the weather forecast, don't go alone if possible, and listen to gut instincts when something doesn't feel right.

One of the most powerful statements I have ever heard about having humility for the disease was expressed by a colleague and good friend of mine, TK. It happened in a group we co-facilitated years ago and gives me chills every time I retell it. For many years of his early adulthood, TK had struggled with cocaine and alcohol but was able to get help, and he'd since attained over fifty years of sobriety. He is well-known in his recovery fellowship, has counseled hundreds of families and clients, and even had his own treatment program. In one therapy group, he told attendees, "If you put a line of cocaine in front of me right now, I can't guarantee I won't snort it." After decades of sobriety and everything he stood to lose, he still couldn't trust the "terrorist in the home." We need to respect the disease's power, and never underestimate its expertise.

For me, the best analogy about always respecting the disease relates to how I approach competitions. If I ever disrespect the capabilities of the person on the other side of the Jiu-Jitsu mat, I have the potential to find myself in a compromising, full-mounted position or tapping out from a guillotine or triangle choke—both very humbling outcomes. Occasionally, an opponent may possess greater proficiency but to best prepare for the fight, I need to keep evolving my game and finding new methods of defense and offense.

As mentioned earlier, some of the most fear-invoking emotions I experience as a clinician working with people in treatment or at any stage of recovery is when they utter the words, "I got this." At face value, these three words may seem to convey a level of positive, healthy self-confidence especially for a person who has felt disempowered for so long. It may appear that treatment has reinvigorated them with a renewed sense of inner strength. But this statement can be tricky, if people are underestimating what they're up against. By respecting the capabilities of the disease with humility, your loved ones will naturally find ways to manage their conditions, such as staying close to healthy fellowships, surrounding themselves with people who will hold them accountable, and continually doing things to strengthen their recovery program.

What a person with a <u>low</u> degree of humility may sound like:

I got this. I don't need my medications anymore. My depression is all gone now!

I can control my (insert substance of choice).

My past sexual traumas are not a problem, as long as I don't think or talk about them.

Heroin was my problem drug. I can manage my Xanax use.

What a person with a <u>high</u> degree of humility may sound like:

I know my addiction is always going to be a factor and need to stay close to my fellowship.

My manic episodes are destructive, so taking meds is critical in my everyday life.

My old patterns of harming myself scare me. I need to practice my self-soothing skills.

Openness to direction

This is the last component of my H2O vaccine, along with honesty and humility. Having Openness to Direction (OTD) means being open to recommendations, feedback, and instructions. As is the case with anything in life, if we haven't resolved something for a long period of time or after multiple attempts, we must be humble enough to realize that what we've been doing hasn't been working, and it's time to change the strategy. People in substance recovery often define insanity as doing the same thing over and over again, expecting different results.

Whether it be on an individual or familial level, having OTD is essential, as it allows room for evolving perspectives and opportunities to implement new ways of doing things, especially if there has been a lack of progress in past attempts. Families willing to make the necessary adjustments and try new recommendations dramatically increase the chances of getting their unwell family members help. These recommendations can come from a therapist, interventionist, clinician, medical provider, or anyone versed in mental health and/or addiction.

Families often seem relieved when I tell them to let myself and the treatment team take over being the "mean, unreasonable, or strict ones" (words the manipulative aspect of the disease may utter to family members to get them to cosign their early departure from treatment). In many ways, the entire family is in treatment (e.g., working on healthy roles, taking share of accountability, educating themselves, changing patterns, etc.). A big part of success relies on being OTD with the treatment team. This approach is not suggesting the family has been weak or can no longer set boundaries; it merely acknowledges what the family has been doing hasn't been working, and possibly a new strategy is needed. The type of language I tell families to use with their loved ones when there is a disagreement about the aftercare plan or some other aspect of treatment is, *"We are all in our own treatment and realize what we have been doing all this time isn't working. We must be open to recommendations from others, such as the treatment team, and what they believe is best for you and the family. If they believe you not coming straight home after treatment is the best option to maximize your success, we will support that recommendation."*

As mentioned above, this strategy of deferring to the treatment team doesn't mean the family is relinquishing empowerment but merely respecting the capabilities of the disease and recognizing the need to have humility and OTD during the treatment process. Furthermore, this approach eliminates the power struggle between families and their recovering members. I have yet to see a client yell at the treatment team regarding a recommendation. They may be upset for a moment but will move into acceptance over time. As they get healthier, they usually end up understanding the rationale behind the recommendations.

Openness to direction also requires your loved ones to be willing to surround themselves with healthy people beyond the treatment team and to remain consistently in touch with others who are conducive to their recovery (e.g., healthy peers, romantic partners, colleagues, etc.). This is an important element of a strong recovery program. Healthy people can provide recommendations, feedback, and directions to your loved ones, especially when they are straying off course. This propensity toward OTD will not allow the disease to isolate your loved ones. They will have people around to reel them back in when they are veering from the recovery program or displaying behaviors (e.g., dishonesty, irritability, isolation, blaming, etc.) that hint at heading down an unhealthy path.

What a person with a <u>low</u> degree of openness to direction (OTD) may sound like:

I can do it my way.

I hear what you're saying, but I know what I'm doing

Yes, I have struggled with relapse in the past, but this time will be different, so I will go with my gut instincts.

All I need is (insert old unhealthy people, places, and situations) and everything will be better.

What a person with a <u>high</u> degree of openness to direction (OTD) may sound like:

I need to follow my therapist's recommendations because I have tendencies to isolate myself and do things on my own when I'm in an unhealthy state.

My psychiatrist says I need to take my anti-psychotic medications and even if I don't want to, I will take them to stay healthy.

I don't want to go to sober living after treatment, but I will if the treatment team thinks it is best.

I firmly believe H2O (Humility, Honesty, Openness to Direction) will benefit anyone in any area of life, whether it be career, social, athletic, health, interpersonal, spiritual, personal, or recovery. As you recall, I grew up playing competitive tennis and was constantly looking for ways to enhance my game. I was always honest with my coach about my areas of deficiency (e.g., net game and second serves). We worked on those first to avoid having those areas exploited during matches. I also tried to stay humble and never underestimate my opponents and whatever arsenal they had in their game (e.g., serve and volley or frequent change of ball pace). Any of these could throw my game off and defeat me. Lastly, I worked on openness to direction with my parents, coaches, and peers, taking in all feedback as "data points."

This same H2O model has also served me well as a clinician, as I am always trying to be a better therapist than the day before. I utilize every individual session, group meeting, treatment team gathering, continuing education seminar, news story, etc., as data I can use to improve my craft. I'm a persistent hunter of feedback and learning opportunities, as I know they make me better. This idea of continuous learning comes from a famous quote in martial arts practice, "A Master thinks like a beginner, always learning."

I challenge you to think of anyone you admire or who has attained a great deal of success in their craft. I guarantee that in addition to having inner fight and determination, that person harbors a high degree of honesty with themselves (e.g., recognizing own strengths and areas of needed development), humility (e.g., respecting the competition and challenges), and openness to direction (e.g., maintaining mentorship).

There you have it, H2O! I guarantee your recovering family members will be successful for life if they diligently practice these three attributes in their daily lives. In my clinical experiences across all settings, these are the most robust, protective factors of people who are successful in recovery. Also, it is stated in the substance abuse recovery arena that willingness is essential in the path towards sobriety. Most definitely, willingness is a big factor to maintaining sobriety and a strong recovery, but I leave it out of H2O, because if someone is demonstrating honesty, humility, and openness to direction, I believe they have a great deal of willingness.

By contrast, I can also nearly guarantee that unwell, struggling family members are most likely deficient in one or more of the three factors of H2O. I teach clients to rank their H2O daily on a Likert Rating scale: 1 (very low degree) to 10 (very high degree). I tell them if they ever dip below a 9 on any of these three, they need to do what they can within their best, diligent efforts to get back to a 9 or 10 as soon as possible. For example, if a person is struggling with being honest, they need to strive to be fully truthful, because their disease becomes heightened when they start harboring secrets. If your loved one hides something (e.g., thinking more about getting high, guilt over a past behavior, not discussing psychotic symptoms, etc.) from their therapists, that secret may lead to a dark place eventually. Secrets related to the disease should be revealed as soon as possible.

In terms of humility, people shouldn't take their struggles for granted. For example, someone with bipolar disorder may feel they can manage their manic symptoms on their own and decide to wean themselves off prescribed medications. Not surprisingly, soon they will find themselves in a full-blown manic episode. I have seen this exact scenario unfold many times.

Often people who struggle with openness to direction may think their way is better and resist a therapist or treatment team's recommendations (e.g., not going back to work full-time immediately after residential treatment, due to the possible negative impact of high levels of stress). The struggling person may feel they are stabilizing with their mental health condition but going back to a job too prematurely can lead to a relapse (e.g., panic attack, nervous break-down, manic episode, substance use to relieve their stress, etc.).

Figure 6 shows that whenever someone dips below a 9 for any aspect of H2O, they should get back to a 9 or 10 as soon as possible. Certainly, a rating of 9 or 10 on all three is desired. As long as they (and the family) are continually self-assessing H2O throughout the recovery journey, their chances for long-term success are greatly maximized.

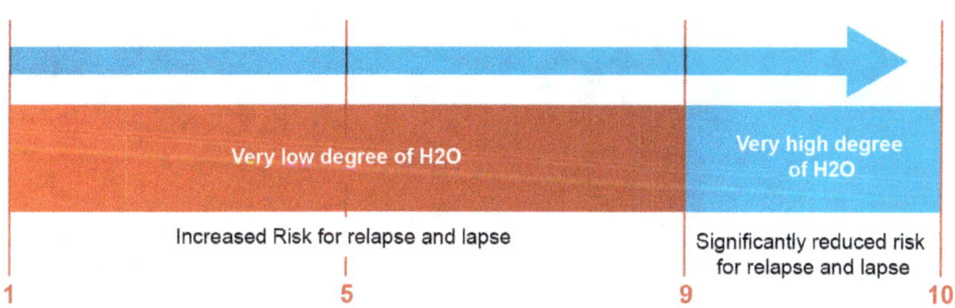

Figure 6. H2O (Honesty, Humility, Openness to Direction) Rating Scale

Chapter 6
Flattening the Risk Curve

This chapter will discuss my risk curve and provide a visual representation of the effects on the shape of the curve when comparing the number of risk factors versus protective factors. The lessening of risk factors and increasing protective factors is known as flattening the risk curve. Please note, I will also discuss harm reduction as a potential treatment option for flattening the curve. Additionally, Chapter 9 will discuss additional protective factors in more detail.

According to Medicine Net, a *risk factor* is "something that increases a person's chances of developing a disease," while Dictionary.com defines it as a "condition, behavior, or other factor that increases risk." When referring to recovery, a risk factor is any person, place, thing, or situation that increases the occurrence of a relapse or lapse or puts someone at risk for unhealthiness. Contrarily, protective factors are, essentially, the antidote to risk factors and things that mitigate risk and increase chances of attaining a healthier path. According to SAMHSA, *protective factors* are "characteristics associated with a lower likelihood of negative outcomes or that reduce a risk factor's impact." The variables in my risk curve are: 1) The number of risk factors and protective factors (X-axis), and 2) The probability of a relapse or lapse

(Y-axis). My curve assumes a direct relationship between these two variables. For clarification, a direct relationship means that as one variable goes up, the other variable goes up and vice versa. For instance, there is a direct relationship between cigarette smoking (risk factor) and increased probability of heart disease. The more cigarettes a person smokes, the higher the probability that person will be susceptible to heart disease. Some examples of risk factors in regard to mental health and substance abuse are a family history of psychiatric illness, family dysfunction, childhood traumas, past or current tragedies, multiple life stressors, lack of a healthy support network of people or services, limited resources, etc.

On the other hand, my risk curve assumes an indirect relationship between the number of protective factors to the probability of a relapse/lapse. In an inverse relationship (opposite of a direct relationship) when a variable goes up, the other variable goes down and vice versa. As an example, an inverse relationship exists between the number of protective factors someone has and the probability of acquiring a bacterial infection. The more protective factors a person practices (e.g., good hygiene habits, social distancing, and use of protective equipment) the lower the probability of contracting a bacterial infection. Some examples of protective factors in regard to mental health and addiction are healthy support systems, healthy coping skills, resilience, strong recovery programs, mindfulness techniques, therapy, treatments, high degree of H2O, etc.

According to Figure 7 below, as the number of risk factors (x-axis) increase (examples in red), the curve gets taller, which means the probability of a relapse or lapse (y-axis) increases. However, as the protective factors (examples in blue) increase, the curve gets flatter which means the probability of a relapse or lapse decreases. Some may argue the actual number of risk factors doesn't matter, because people struggling with addiction or mental health can be put at risk by a sole risk factor. My response would be that one risk factor almost always has other risk factors attached. Therefore, trying to avoid one specific risk factor is not a comprehensive strategy.

Let's use an example of a male who has a family history of substance abuse and has struggled with substances in the past but has been abstinent for three months through what he calls sheer "willpower." If he believes his *only* risk factor is illicit substances and his only strategy is to avoid substances, he is overlooking all the other risk factors associated with his substance use. These factors could be friends he hangs out with who use drugs, lacking a strong support system to hold him accountable, limited coping skills to manage stressors, and being low on H2O—all elements of a weaker recovery program. My point is that simply avoiding a risk factor (e.g., not drinking alcohol) is very important but not good enough. This male would need to increase the number of protective factors to decrease his chances of experiencing a heightened mental health symptom or a relapse or lapse with a substance.

As an aside, a common question I receive from clients and family members in relation to flattening the risk curve involves the continued use of certain substances after treatment. For instance, clients ask whether they can smoke marijuana to take the edge off anxiety, because alcohol was their substance of choice. Parents ask if they need to stop drinking in the home when their child (who struggled with liquor) returns after treatment. Clients inquire whether they should keep their job stocking cases of alcohol at a bar after completing treatment for alcoholism. Some ask if they can still hang out with friends who use substances, if the friends will respect their sobriety.

I tell clients and family members that although I work in addiction treatment, I am not completely against marijuana, alcohol, methylphenidates (ADHD stimulant medications), and painkillers for everyone. Certainly, in the case of illicit substances (e.g., methamphetamines, heroin, cocaine, etc.), I am sternly against their use, no matter the circumstances, because they are illegal and widely known to be life threatening to both medical and mental health. Of course, a legal substance can also be dangerous when abused (e.g., alcohol, opiates, benzodiazepines).

The reason I am not completely against certain substances is because some people can have a glass of wine with their steak, or smoke marijuana to help with insomnia, or take a regimen of pain-killers after surgery or ADHD medications for school or work and not develop a problem. However, when someone has a family history of addiction or has struggled with dependence or a psychiatric con-dition, mind-altering substances can worsen symptoms, make them more sensitive to an underlying psychiatric condition, or bring about the onset of a mental health or medical condition sooner rather than later. Also, this exacerbation of symptoms resulting from substance use exposes them to risk factors (e.g., desire to try other substances, being around people who use substances, or frequenting environments not conducive to recovery). In these cases, using these substances puts people with conditions at a higher risk than someone without these conditions and greatly increases the chances that their condition may become more acute or worsen.

When families inquire whether they should stop drinking in the home, I tell them they should not have to completely alter their life-style but should also realize having substances present in the home puts their recovering family members at greater risk of relapse or lapse. My answer to the question about working at a bar stocking alcohol or hanging out with friends who use substances? Denzel Washington once told a graduating class at the University of Pennsylvania, "The longer you hang around a barber shop, sooner or later you're going to get a haircut." The best way to avoid a situation is to do just that, avoid it. Flattening the curve should always be of primary importance, reducing the risk factors that could lead to trouble while always build-ing the protective factors for extra protection against the disease's capabilities.

The reality is, the curve will never be completely flat, no matter how many protective factors one has and especially if your struggling family members have been challenged for a long time. There will always be some level of potential risk. This goes for all of us with our own diseases. As you recall, I used the metaphor of a radar system. Even with a strong recovery program in place and years of healthy living, the disease will always be somewhere on the outskirts of the radar, waiting for the perfect storm to reinvigorate it. And like my analogy of someone struggling with a history of hypertension, even after years of normal blood pressure due to medication, lifestyle changes, stress management, and a healthy diet, that person will always need to respect the disease of hypertension, as it will flare up again under the perfect circumstances. Likewise, your family members who are struggling with a history of mental health conditions (e.g., anxiety disorders, mood disorders, psychotic disorders, etc.), substance abuse, or addiction (e.g., pills, alcohol, gambling, sex, eating, etc.) are no exception. There will always be a risk curve for them. Their lifelong goal will be flattening the curve to lower the risk of heightened manifestations of the disease such as a relapse, lapse, or worsening of symptoms as well as increasing the probability of reaching a crisis level.

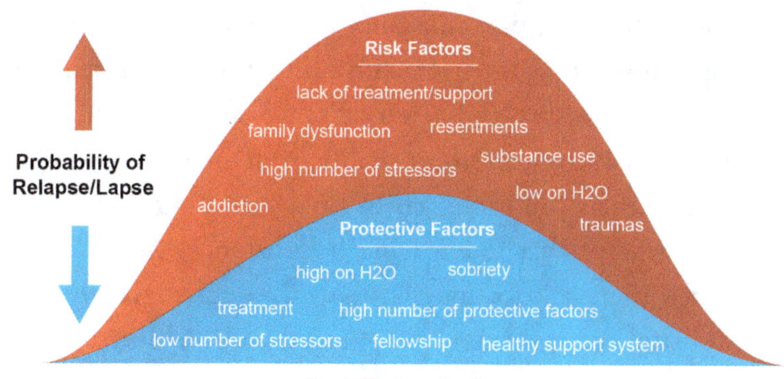

Figure 7. Relapse and Lapse Risk Curve

Complete abstinence vs. harm reduction

An important consideration in our discussion is whether complete abstinence from non-prescribed and mind-altering substances is the only way, or whether harm reduction is a viable option. Moreover, is harm reduction an acceptable course of action for flattening the risk curve?

As I have stated, this book is mainly targeted for families who have attempted nearly everything to obtain guidance. They have attempted interventions with their struggling loved one and are at a level of desperation, as deleterious consequences may result if they do not get their loved one help sooner than later. On the individual level, this book was intended for people who have chronically struggled with mental health and/or substance abuse and at a severe level (e.g., over-doses, suicide attempts, psychotic episodes). These individuals may have already attempted alternative measures, such as using less of their problematic substance or transitioning to "less dangerous" substance options as a form of reducing harm (e.g., smoking marijuana instead of heroin, lessening wine consumption, switching to beer from hard liquor). Earlier, I stated that people who have a mental health condition and/or a current or past substance abuse issue are at greater risk when using substances. Moreover, consuming non-prescribed, mind-altering substances has a high likelihood of worsening existing mental health symptoms, increasing susceptibility to an underlying condition, or exasperating their condition. For people struggling at this level of severity, my belief is that re-engaging in substances would dramatically heighten their risk for moving towards a crisis level; therefore, complete abstinence is strongly encouraged and the only option for people at this level of struggle.

On the other hand, harm reduction may be an option in one's treatment plan, depending on the needs of the individual and the severity of their condition. According to the National Harm Reduction Coalition, harm reduction is "a set of practical strategies and ideas aimed at reducing negative consequences associated with drug use. Harm reduction incorporates a spectrum of strategies that includes safer use, managed use, abstinence, meeting people who use drugs 'where they're at,' and addressing conditions of use along with the use itself."

Please note: harm reduction can also be applied to alcohol use and not only to drugs as well as other behaviors related to mental health that may cause significant harm to a person (e.g., suicidal behaviors or self-inflicted bodily harm). For instance, pinching instead of using a razor blade to cut one's arm, hitting a punching bag rather than a brick wall, or holding ice cubes instead of pulling out one's hair are all examples of harm reduction for behaviors beyond substance use as they all mimic some form of cathartic relief while lessening the extent of bodily harm.

In relation to substance abuse issues, I am open to the idea of harm reduction, especially if a person is working closely with a medical provider (i.e., Medication Assisted Treatment (MAT)) and therapist. I am more receptive when it's used for individuals who have not tried that route before, and who will not be put at extreme risk if continuing to use substances. However, if harm reduction has been tried multiple times to no avail or even created worse outcomes as a result (e.g., a person relapsed to the same degree or to a more severe level), I would not encourage it. In these cases, complete abstinence would be the recommended path.

An example of a harm reduction tactic may be a person who has a history of panic attacks and severe alcohol use. To offset withdrawal symptoms such as insomnia, angry outbursts, and irritability due to alcohol abstinence, this person may smoke marijuana as a way to mitigate these symptoms. A second example of a harm reduction strategy would be someone who drinks alcohol excessively but may begin to consume drinks with less alcohol percent content, dilute alcohol with fruit juices, or set limits on drinking to avoid intoxication, or limit the number of days per week they will drink. A last example of a harm reduction treatment plan can be the use of an opioid antagonist such as Suboxone for individuals who abuse heroin or other opiates (e.g., pain killers, morphine, fentanyl). In this case, a medical provider closely monitors the patient with aims to gradually lessen the opioid antagonist use over time.

Again, harm reduction can be an effective approach but should be attempted in collaboration with a trained professional who can closely monitor the use. Please talk to your treatment team for more guidance on this alternative approach.

Chapter 7

My Phases of Recovery

This chapter will introduce my phases of recovery model. Hopefully, at this point of the process, your loved ones have agreed to seek help and enter a treatment program. If you are at this juncture, you successfully united as a family, maintained a unified vision, and executed your strategic plan.

My model will outline what generally takes place during each segment of the recovery process and some of the most significant issues that can arise in each phase. Figure 8 illustrates the trajectory of the recovery process.

If you recall, treatment is defined as the actual process of attaining interventional services such as residential, inpatient, or intensive outpatient treatment, or some variation of sober, group home, or transitional living. Treatment, at the minimum, will include services such as individual therapy, family therapy, group therapy, additional support groups, and working with a psychiatric medical provider. Recovery will include treatment initially but will not always involve treatment on a long-term basis. Remember, recovery is the overall process of maintaining a healthy lifestyle over a lifetime. For instance, working out regularly at a gym, being part of a church group, volunteering for philanthropy, working a job, and maintaining sobriety are all examples of various activities in recovery.

I decided to develop my phases of recovery model after both family members and clients consistently asked questions about the treatment and recovery processes. Some of these questions evolved around uncertainty about next steps; often clients wonder why they can't go back to their regular lifestyle right after treatment. Their varied and numerous questions included, "Why aren't you supporting me to return home after treatment? Aren't I much better now?" "What do we do next after this stage of residential treatment?" "We are not ready for our son to come back home this soon. Where can we send him for aftercare to stabilize even more?" "Why don't my parents trust me? I've been sober for three weeks!" "Why does my daughter still have suicidal thoughts when she has been in treatment for thirty days?" "How come my son still has cravings for marijuana when he has not used it in months?" "Why am I still anxious after all of the medications prescribed and mindfulness techniques taught in treatment?" "When are my depressed thoughts going to end? I've been in treatment and therapy for six months!"

All of these are completely valid questions. People tend to believe the treatment and recovery process end once they feel better and reach their immediate goals, or when treatment is finished. But recovery is a life-long journey, one which involves constantly improving the "recovery game." I remind families and clients that treatment is only one component, albeit a critical one in the recovery journey.

My phases of recovery model presents an overall view of the different phases of treatment and recovery, so you can get an idea of what the journey may look like.

Before we go further, it's best I define these terms: *structure, routine,* and *accountability*. All are critical elements in a recovery program and will be mentioned again in later chapters. Then, I will define some of the most typical options in the early treatment process.

Structure

One of the most important elements of treatment is a great deal of structure, which means organization and order. During treatment and in a proficient or credentialed program, clients typically have a daily schedule, with organized time for certain activities and goals to be achieved. These goals can include individual therapy sessions, attendance in therapy groups, family sessions, outside support groups for sobriety, medicine management, meals, gym workouts, leisure time, experiential activities, etc. With structure, people in treatment know what they will be doing, and nearly every hour of the day is accounted for. This high level of structure may not be realistic (e.g., having staff wake them up, ensure they take their meds, hold them accountable to attend meetings, etc.) when they leave treatment, but it teaches the importance of starting each day with direction and focus. People often struggle when they wake up, not knowing what's to come or what to do. Your recovering family members will become accustomed to structure, realize its importance, and hopefully, make it a familiar way of life after they leave treatment. Please note, without structure, boredom can set in, and boredom has a strong relationship to relapse or lapse. In his book *Atomic Habits*, author James Clear states, "Boredom is perhaps the greatest villain on the quest for self-improvement."

Routine

Another essential part of recovery is routine. Routine is a fixed sequence of activities which are repeated. Structure and routine have similarities, and there are some distinctions. I view routine as more personalized, consisting of activities within the framework of structure that are frequently performed, likely on a daily basis. For instance, in treatment, clients may have their own routine activities within the built-in structure of the day (e.g., meditating in the morning before breakfast, working on therapy work during free time, taking an evening shower after dinner, having a specific workout regimen during gym time, etc.). After treatment, they can add to their routines, making them more personalized for their needs. Again, routine also prevents the inherent dangers in boredom and can provide purpose and direction in your loved ones' daily lives. The philosopher Aristotle once said, "We are what we repeatedly do," while motivational coach and speaker Eric Thomas advised, "Wake up with a purpose. Don't wake up like an accident." These men speak to the importance of routine for all of us. We need to be aware how impactful structure and routine can be for those in early recovery.

Accountability

A third major element of a strong recovery program is accountability. Accountability is the entities or system that holds clients responsible and keeps them adhering to their recovery program. Accountability can come in the form of healthy people, places, situations, and things. These persons or entities should have the motivation and ability to keep clients strong on H20 (Honesty, Humility, Openness to Direction).

Some examples of sources of accountability can be people (e.g., therapist, physician, sobriety sponsor, life coach, recovery fellowship, family unit), places (e.g., workplace, church, sobriety meetings), situations (e.g., household responsibilities, duty caring for family members, financial obligations), and things (e.g., pets, house, finances). It is strongly recommended that clients have at least three to five people, at minimum, to whom they will be accountable. These should be people who can look at your recovering family members with an objective lens without worrying about hurting their feelings. They should be sources for honest, straightforward feedback. If, prior to discharge, a client identifies a father, mother, sister, brother, or grandmother for accountability, I am concerned about objectivity. These relatives may be loving, supportive people but hesitant to give honest feedback for fear of hurting feelings or because of how their interactions may affect other people in the family. It is more difficult for family members to look through an objective lens when providing feedback to their recovering family members. I advise clients to count family members (if healthy and conducive to a strong recovery program) as one, collective entity, and find a minimum of two to four more people who will hold them accountable.

Now, please allow me to briefly define some of the various treatment options I have mentioned earlier in the book, as they are critical components in my Phases of Recovery. Please contact your medical provider, social worker, therapist, or treatment professional if you need more information.

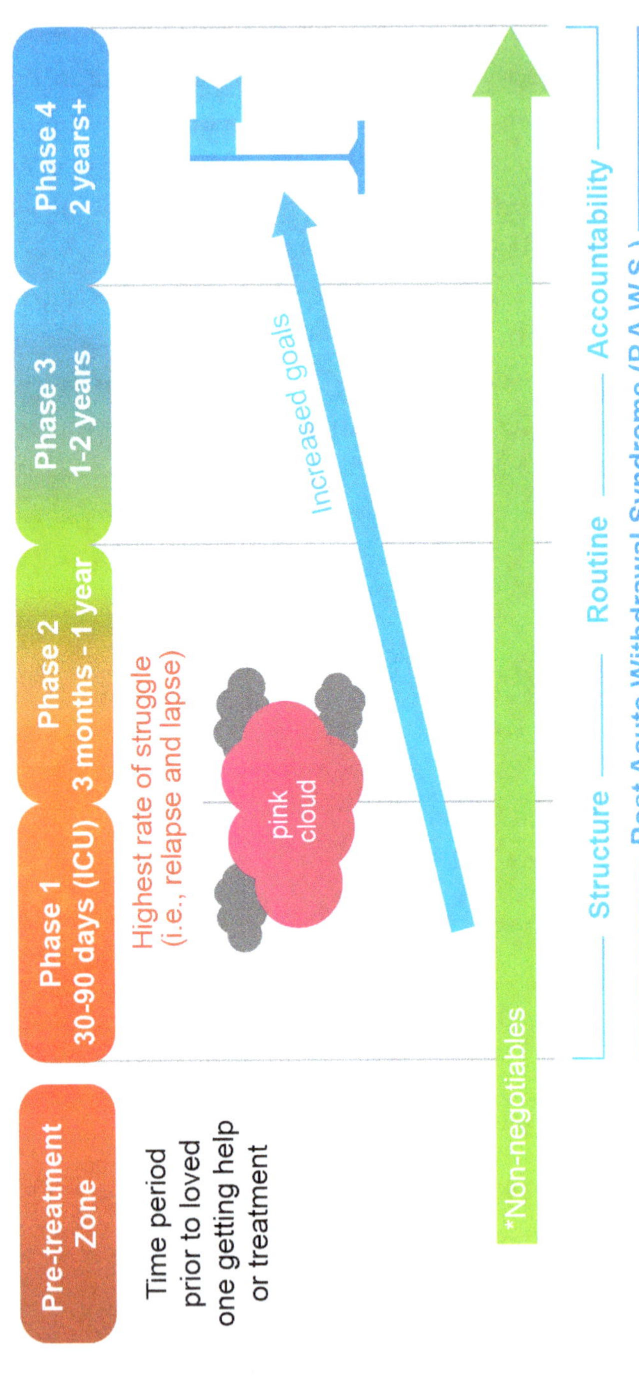

Figure 8. Phases of Recovery

Please note, the following treatment options pertain to those struggling with mental health conditions and/or substance abuse issues:

- Detox facility/detoxification is a place prioritizing medical care for a person needing close medical supervision and medicine management to clear substances from their body and prevent significant withdrawal symptoms from substances such as alcohol, benzodiazepines, opiates, etc. A detox facility may be necessary prior to the next level of care (e.g. residential).

- Inpatient hospitalization takes place in a psychiatric hospital setting and is typically needed when a person is an imminent danger to themselves or others or is gravely disabled and requires intensive care and supervision prior to a step-down level of care (e.g. residential or outpatient treatment).

- Residential treatment is a live-in healthcare facility (more of a home environment rather than a hospital setting) where clients receive twenty-four-hour care and supervision. Included in this setting are psychiatric medicine management, group therapy, individual therapy, and experiential activities.

- Partial hospitalization program (PHP) is similar in many regards to residential treatment in that it offers intensive care, a structured schedule (usually Monday through Friday, 8:00 a.m. to 5:00 p.m.) and supervision, but the clients return to their own residence or a sober living facility each day. PHP is viewed as a step-down level of care from residential.

- Intensive outpatient program (IOP), generally speaking, is a step-down level of care from PHP and doesn't require the same intense level of treatment and structure. Clients may meet several days a week for less hours (e.g. 4:00 p.m. to 7:00 p.m.) and return to their place of residence. Initially, IOP may start with five days a week and lessen in frequency over time as the client gets healthier.

- Individual therapy refers to a treatment option in which a person meets with a mental health therapist weekly or less frequently based on the needs and goals of the client.
- A sobriety coach is a person who supports a person's path of sobriety and can provide support and a level of accountability.

Now, we are ready to begin talking about the different phases of recovery. Throughout, I will explain how structure, routine, and accountability fit into the process and what treatment options are generally involved in each phase.

**Pre-treatment
Zone**

The first part of this book focused on the Pre-treatment Zone. In this stage, your unwell family members have refused to get help and you are engulfed with panic, fear, confusion, guilt, anxiety, and hopelessness. This is the stage where you need to strategically implement plans to release yourself from guilt, accept the inevitable consequences of untreated mental health and substance use, share equal accountability, be firm with the non-negotiables, set your loved ones up to a point of desperation, and plant emotional seeds to let them know you will continue to love and care for them on their path to a healthier lifestyle.

In Chapter 8, we will go into further detail, breaking down the steps needed in this stage to get help for your struggling family members.

**Phase 1
30-90 days (ICU)**

Phase 1 lasts about thirty to ninety days. In Phase 1, an unwell person has agreed to enter a treatment program. This treatment phase can occur after they were placed in an involuntary or voluntary hospitalization stay due to heightened acuity, because of concern they were an imminent danger to themselves or others, or because they became gravely disabled. If you recall, people who are forced into treatment can be equally successful as people who enter willingly and voluntarily, especially as they stabilize and move towards a healthier baseline level of functioning.

Treatment in Phase 1 would typically entail a residential treatment program due to the urgency of help needed, where clients live under the care of a facility or program which involves a high degree of structure, routine, and accountability. There may be other variations to treatment at this phase, such as an IOP or living in a sober living level of care.

In general, sober living is a residence for people who are working on transitioning back into the community after completing some level of treatment or intensive care. The sober living is aimed at enforcing sobriety and maintaining a strong recovery program, and it also involves supervision of an agency along with a staff house manager. There is a higher degree of structure, routine, and accountability in the sober living capacity, but not to the degree maintained in a residential treatment program. Sober living households provide a person with increased individual autonomy, a more individualized recovery program created by the client, and more liberties (e.g., access to phones, cars, ability to work, managing own medications, less restrictive curfews, etc.). However, chronically struggling people who have been resistant to help and who have never been in a residential level of care may now require a higher level of care due to the heightened level of crisis. I've seen the highest success rates when clients remain in a residential or intensive level of care for at least ninety days. A step-down range of care in Phase 2 can include a PHP, an IOP, individual therapy, group therapy, sober living, support group meetings, etc. I'll explain more about this idea below.

Phase 1 closely resembles the Intensive Care Unit (ICU) of a hospital. Remember, people in an ICU are not thinking about anything other than stabilization and survival. Of course, the situation with someone in a hospital ICU (e.g., intubation, induced coma, critical condition) is different in many respects to my model's Phase I ICU, but the overarching acuity of struggles and the need for immediate stabilization is similarly critical. People in Phase 1 may have been in serious danger and at risk of experiencing deleterious consequences. Some people in Phase 1 may be recovering from a recent suicide attempt, an overdose on substances, or currently experiencing a psychotic episode or a severely depressed state.

During Phase 1, people are most likely to leave treatment prematurely and eventually relapse or lapse, due to the drastic changes taking place. This is why family members have to do whatever it takes to keep them in this first phase of treatment. As mentioned in Chapter 4, *Must Know #23* Post-Acute Withdrawal Syndrome (PAWS) is most intense during this early stage of treatment and can cause a great deal of physical discomfort and emotional distress. Some of these changes your loved one will experience include adjusting to new medications, withdrawing from substances, experiencing heightened symptoms, distress from being away from their regular environment, separating from family members, being surrounded by other acute clients, having fears and anxiety about the future, etc.

In some cases, people have made major turnarounds in Phase 1 of treatment due to the interventions involved in treatment such as sobriety, medication management, healthier eating and sleeping patterns, and various therapies. I told you about a client who initially had plans to hurt his family but after a few weeks of sobriety and medications, re-established a loving connection with them. I have witnessed clients come to treatment at the height of their unhealthiness, wanting nothing but to die, but then recognizing the value in living as they got healthier. I have also worked with clients experiencing psychosis and watched these symptoms greatly lessen once they were on a medication regimen. Clients struggling with massive panic attacks have stabilized and improved as they attained healthier coping skills and were no longer surrounded by stressors. Many positive changes can occur in Phase 1 of treatment. It may be one of the roughest and most uncomfortable times in the early treatment process, but it's extremely critical to trust in the process and allow room to change and grow during this period.

Pink Cloud Effect

In the first few days or weeks of treatment, sometimes clients experience a jolt of positivity, energy, and euphoria (intense feelings of happiness). This is called the Pink Cloud Effect. You may experience it as a jubilant phone call from your loved one in a facility, or you might witness their intense, happy feelings in a preliminary family session. Examples of this language can be, "Dad and Mom, I am so done with (Insert drug of choice)!" "I am ready to go home. My depression is much better now." "Things are perfect. Once I go back to work, I will never revert back to this old life." These feelings aren't bad; they are great. I tell family members to validate their loved ones when they are feeling this way, encourage them to stick with the program and realize that treatment is a process, and motivate them to continue to get better—rather than telling them, "This is all the Pink Cloud Effect." Positivity and support are key.

The reality is, a series of dark clouds (e.g., anxiety, depression, anger, resentments, substance cravings, repressed traumas, or unresolved grief and loss, etc.) is lurking closely behind the Pink Cloud. The emergence of the Pink Cloud in the first few weeks of treatment makes perfect sense. Your loved ones are taking medications, maintaining abstinence from substances, sleeping better, eating three meals a day, connecting with peers, talking about their struggles in therapy, etc. When families witness the Pink Cloud, I suggest they use validation such as, *We are so happy and proud of you! You sound great and appear to be making progress already. Let's stick with this process and use this opportunity to continue to grow and change.* When your loved one has been in and out of treatment before, I advise family members to add, *we have been here before, and the situation became challenging because we didn't stick with the process. Let's give it more time to build on this positive change.* This positive reinforcement of noticeable changes provides hope, optimism, and encouragement to keep pushing forward and remain engaged in the treatment process.

I cannot emphasize enough how vital Phase 1 is in the early recovery process. It is the foundation for healing, allowing the family unit to rebuild itself by creating healthier dynamics. That is why families must keep their unwell family members in this phase as long as possible (this is assuming, of course, they are not in imminent danger, and the program is not egregious or negligent with care). If your family members decide to jump ship and discharge prematurely, your language should be clear and concise and sound something like, *you have every right to leave. Just note, we will not support you, and you are on your own. You will not be able to come home or get any help from us, because we will be doing you more harm than good. We love you and want you to get healthy.* When families or the support system hold firm to these boundaries, limiting a client's viable options, over ninety percent end up staying in treatment due to the unpleasantness of other options (e.g., homelessness, jail, hospital, not having basic needs, etc.).

Typical goals clients are working on in Phase 1 include adjusting to a medication regimen, engaging in various therapies, attaining healthy coping skills, working on healthy relationships and communication with family members, establishing fellowship in sobriety support groups, and maintaining a high degree of structure, routine, and accountability. Please note, there are some clients who still need more than thirty to ninety days to stabilize due to the acuity of their struggles. Therefore, a longer period working on Phase 1 level of goals may be necessary. This has occurred perhaps ten to twenty percent of the time with clients I have worked with in treatment. Approximately eighty to ninety percent of the time, clients are appropriate for Phase 2 level of goals after thirty to ninety days, when they have a stronger recovery program in place. It is best to work closely with the treatment team to come up with the best treatment plan.

**Phase 2
3 months - 1 year**

Phase 2 lasts from about three months to one year. At this point, clients have successfully completed Phase 1 of treatment. Families are beginning to feel relieved and hopeful, as some clients may have never logged in this much sobriety time or healthiness before. I have known numerous clients who, prior to treatment, had never experienced more than one week of abstinence since they started using substances. For them, and for all, thirty to ninety days of treatment and sobriety is a major feat that should be recognized, validated, and capitalized on.

Please note: although the higher range of treatment for Phase 2 can last up to one year, I (along with many clinicians I've collaborated with) believe that one year is still considered early recovery. In the initial year, an abundance of growth, change, and healing can take place, especially if clients had been hospitalized due to psychotic features, an overdose, suicidality, nervous breakdown, homelessness, manic episode, or some other highly acute condition or circumstance. In these cases, it will take a minimum of one year's time for major healing to occur. Finalizing a diagnosis, finding the right medications, and achieving the optimum dosage levels can also take a good deal of time. There is the possibility that an accurate psychiatric diagnosis may not be rendered, as this process can take months or even years to finalize. The diagnosis process is even more complicated when a substance is involved because a period of abstinence is needed to understand if the symptoms (e.g., psychosis, depression, anxiety, panic attacks, etc.) are due to the substances, or an underlying mental health condition. Please note: DNA genetic swab tests are available which may assist psychiatric providers when developing a medication treatment plan for your loved ones (i.e., what medications clients metabolize better than others). There are varying opinions on the usefulness of these tests across medical providers, but they may be worth exploring, especially for loved ones who have tried numerous iterations of medication plans and/or struggle with medication compliance. Also, by narrowing the number of medication options, families can prevent loved ones from getting frustrated, abandoning all medication treatment when they have to undergo too many combinations of prescriptions with little to no improvements and/or enduring heightened, debilitating side effects. Talk to your psychiatric provider for more information.

As I mentioned, Phase 1 is similar - to a degree - to hospitalization in an ICU. Stabilization and survival are the main goals. When someone is released from a hospital ICU, an immediate return to the same life after discharge is not usually the recommended course of treatment. The same goes for clients completing Phase 1 of treatment. To maximize long-term success, a step-down level of care is optimal, making Phase 2 a critical period in recovery. For instance, someone admitted to the ICU for a massive stroke would not be advised to return to the same lifestyle (e.g., long job hours, multiple gym visits per week, extensive travel) after discharge. The best recommendation is a step-down level of continued care as indicated, such as physical rehabilitation, speech therapy, cognitive therapy, occupational therapy, etc. This same model is used for people transitioning out of Phase 1 of treatment. To maximize the best possible outcomes, a step-down continuance of care that maintains a higher degree of structure, routine, and accountability is highly recommended.

Countless times, I have witnessed clients leave the forty-five-to-ninety-day residential program and struggle with the transition back home, because they became accustomed to the structure and routine in place. This systematic, organized lifestyle had become their norm. A step-down range of care in Phase 2 can include a partial hospitalization program, an intensive outpatient program, individual therapy, group therapy, sober living, support group meetings, etc. This strategy serves as a warm transition or a softer landing approach. Early on in Phase 2, I have seen clients attend session with a "deer in the headlights" look, somewhat in shock about how different the lifestyle is, even when transitioning under the same umbrella of a treatment facility (e.g., from a treatment facility's residential program down to its intensive outpatient program). These clients discuss how different life is without prepared meals and the assistance of staff, who ensure they take their meds, wake them up on time, and hold them accountable to attend sessions. Also, when clients immediately return home (especially if they live alone), work the same number of hours at their job, take a full-time school load, or jump back into the exact same lifestyle, old triggers may still be present. Sometimes, interaction with people in those places or some situations may not be healthy and conducive to a strong recovery program.

This doesn't mean clients have to wait exactly one year before they can go back to work full-time or take a full course load at school. They are encouraged to work with a treatment team or therapist to come up with the best plan appropriate to their recovery. Everyone presents with varying needs, strengths, resources, and conditions, so a case-by-case approach is warranted.

In reality, I have observed that people start to experience major changes and growth after being in an intensive level of care for at least six months (e.g., residential care + PHP + IOP). The remaining six months of the one-year timeframe in Phase 2 will still require a higher degree of structure, routine, and accountability, but those people can start taking on some of the higher-level goals that will be discussed in Phase 3 and 4.

Phase 1 and Phase 2 are the most vulnerable time periods, during which people are most likely to experience relapse or lapses, so it's imperative to maintain a structured recovery plan. Family members also need this amount of time to work on themselves and make necessary changes. The span of an entire year may be necessary for clients to create a new fellowship with healthy people in their support network and to solidify a clearer path (e.g., school, career, financial, relationships). If there are grief or loss issues to address, it may take a year of intensive work to reach acceptance. Furthermore, though less frequent in Phase 2, the Pink Cloud can show up in some form, manifesting in an overconfident "I got this" mentality, which is why it's imperative to maintain firm boundaries and support their continued path of recovery.

When clients make it to the one-year mark, they greatly improve their chances for long-term success. That doesn't mean they are done with the healing process after one year; recovery is a lifelong journey. But it does mean they navigated through some of the toughest storms in the treatment process, and this bodes well for their chances for long-term success.

Typical goals that clients work on in Phase 2 are transitioning to a step-down level of care (e.g., sober living, group home), working part-time at a job that is conducive to healthy living, attending school part-time, participating in volunteer work, continuing to establish fellowship in sobriety support groups, and maintaining a moderately high degree of structure, routine, and accountability. In my work with clients, about twenty percent still require Phase 2 level of care after six months or one year. At least eighty percent of clients at this stage are appropriate for Phase 3. Again, it is important to collaborate with a treatment team (e.g., psychiatrist, therapist, case manager, social worker, etc.) to devise the best course of action to meet the individual's needs.

Phase 3
1-2 years

Phase 3 lasts approximately one to two years. At this phase of the recovery process, families are starting to feel much more hopeful about their loved one's prognosis. Also, by this time, clients are starting to more closely resemble the people their families knew before their struggles. They look healthier, sound more confident, and may begin to pursue higher-level goals. They may even emanate an energy that resembles optimism. Great work on everyone's part if you've arrived at this phase!

Of course, recovery is a lifelong journey, so the work isn't ever finished. But at this phase, the process is starting to become more automatic and routine. Clients are getting more comfortable managing their mental health and sobriety, and they have a foundational skillset to manage stressors. Hopefully, they're also starting to realize what a healthy lifestyle has to offer. The family can take care of their own responsibilities, sleep better, spend time with other loved ones, etc. Some typical treatment options at this phase are individual therapy and sobriety meetings. In some cases in which a person may still need more structure, routine, and accountability, an intensive outpatient program may still be appropriate.

It is important to note that in Phase 3, clients may still be experiencing the effects of PAWS, but less frequently and less intensely. The typical PAWS symptoms I observe in clients during Phase 3 are an ebb and flow of anxiety, feelings of mild sadness, occasional cravings for substances, various types of stress, and an ongoing desire to rebuild trust with family. At this point, structure, routine, and accountability are still essential and important, but perhaps can be loosened a bit.

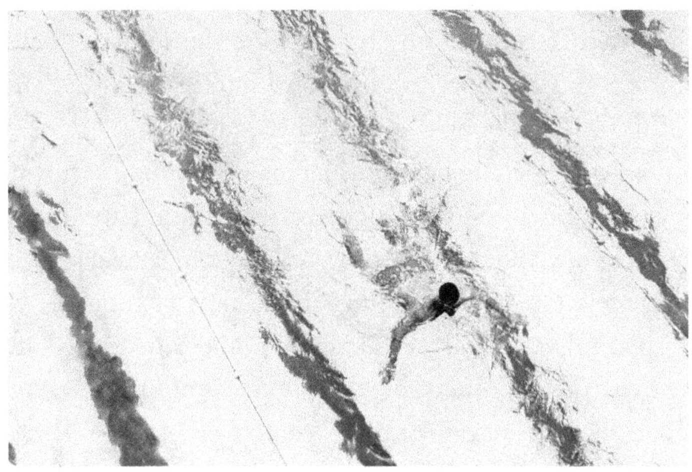

The image I like to use when explaining this concept of less rigidity in structure and routine is that of a competition swimming pool. Each lane is separated by floating dividers. The dividers provide structure and operate as a border, so swimmers don't stray out of their lane. The lane also provides direction, holding the competitors accountable to stay in their designated space to avoid disqualification. This swimming lane closely resembles the structure, routine, and accountability necessary in the treatment and recovery process. The lane is still there in Phase 3, but it has widened. Early in Phase 1 and 2, the lanes were narrow, not allowing much wiggle room. This rigidity was essential because clients weren't in a healthy place. They needed stabilization and weren't at a point to make the best decisions. They also needed a high degree of accountability, with people to watch over and ensure they weren't straying from course. In Phase 3, the lanes are wider, with more room to maneuver as recovery becomes more automatic and with more independence. The boundaries are still present, but the widening represents the ability and capacity for your loved one to take on higher-level goals. At this juncture, survival is not as much of a focus, compared to Phases 1 and 2. Remember, while in Phase 1 (ICU), higher level goals (e.g., going back to work full-time, getting married, taking a full class load, etc.) are not considered, as stabilization and a return to a healthy baseline are the primary focus. Once stabilization and a return to baseline occurs in Phase 3, clients are more equipped to take on more advanced goals.

Typical goals clients take on in Phase 3 include securing a full-time job, living in their own place or with roommates, applying to graduate schools, taking a full-time college course load, and entering a romantic relationship. Assuming clients have a strong recovery program in place, by the end of this timeframe of one to two years, I've observed that about ninety percent or more of clients are mentally and medically ready to transition to Phase 4 of recovery. This estimate takes into account clients who have had few to no lapses, stabilized on a medication regimen (if medications are still needed), and made their recovery program a top priority, even as it is now more routine and automatic.

**Phase 4
2 years+**

Phase 4 lasts two years and beyond. At this stage of the process, it's perfectly okay to be joyful and exceptionally grateful. You and your family have made it this far! It was probably one of the most challenging times of your lives, but through diligent work, by accepting guidance and by keeping hope alive, you stayed in the fight. The family unit is once again full of gratitude, promise, and hopefulness. Worrying day and night about the well-being of your loved ones has become part of a distant past. At this point, recovery is even more automatic, PAWS has an extremely small or no effect, and the person experiences a heightened motivation in life (e.g., pursuing career aspirations, maintaining healthy relationships, serving as a sponsor in the substance abuse recovery arena like AA, sharing own personal story at mental health awareness events to help others, etc.)

As I have mentioned multiple times, recovery is a lifelong journey for everyone. As long as the family unit and support system continue attending to their own recovery processes, looking for new ways to grow, understanding their roles, practicing assertive love, and holding firm to the non-negotiables, the chance of lifelong success is very high.

At this point, the level of structure, routine, and accountability are at a moderate level. The recovery process is automatic, a strong fellowship of healthy people has been established, and even bigger goals are being pursued.

However, I have worked with clients who have struggled, relapsed or lapsed after years or even decades of recovery. Across the board, this can be explained by the following top three reasons: they distanced themselves from their recovery programs, they were low on H2O, and/or they no longer had a healthy fellowship surrounding them. On the other hand, I've had four notable clients who, while in substance recovery, experienced extremely tragic events (i.e., loss of a child via suicide, cancer diagnosis, bankruptcy, and divorce); each claimed their recovery program was the only thing keeping them alive and sober. These real case examples illustrate how powerful recovery can be, even during the most challenging events as it builds the vessel of strong mind and body able to dredge through the roughest of storms.

The goals clients pursue at this stage are similar to the ones in Phase 3 but at even higher levels. Some of these include getting married, having children, starting their own businesses, creating bigger financial goals, traveling more extensively, etc. Typical treatment options at this phase can be individual therapy and sobriety meetings.

There you have it, the stages of recovery, from Phase 1 to Phase 4. Please remember, Phases 1-2 are the most challenging, as this is the period where most changes take place. The first year is the most vulnerable time, and you will be full of doubt and uncertainty about whether your loved ones will give up their old, unhealthy lifestyle while you fight the "waiting for the other shoe to drop" mentality. The family unit also undergoes drastic transformations as the members make major revisions at both individual and group levels. Additionally, everyone is navigating through a great deal of discomfort. As time goes on and healing takes place, everyone begins to understand and accept a clearer vision of what a healthy lifestyle looks like—one many people don't want to give up once they see the beauty life can offer.

Chapter 8
Get Your Loved One into Treatment Step-By Step Plan

This chapter is designed to outline my step-by-step process for identifying, preparing, implementing, and maintaining a strategic plan to get your loved ones out of the Pre-treatment Zone and into Phase 1, and establish a long-term recovery plan.

Figure 9 illustrates the major steps to follow when developing the family plan. This is my method when working with families, from the moment they call for help to the day their unwell family members begin treatment. The steps are designed to help gather and organize important information to use in developing a strategic plan.

It is worth reiterating, this book is designed for struggling loved ones who are refusing any type of help, when sooner-rather-than-later action is deemed necessary to avoid serious consequences. Families at this stage have tried everything to no avail. All attempts to collaborate and partner with the loved one have been exhausted and offered options have been rejected. I mention this because the following plan development does not include input from the loved one, most notably in the Pre-treatment Zone and Phase 1. Once they are more stable and have better insight and decision-making capabilities, they can and should assist in designing their treatment program. This collaboration typically begins to take place from Phase 2 on. As a reminder, these steps are to serve as a guide in developing your plan of action and it's important to consult with a mental health professional for further recommendations.

Lastly, after reading this section, many families may conclude, "This is all easier said than done." I completely validate that sentiment. I firmly believe that the knowledge and concepts embedded in the plan are just that—if they are not carried out and diligently executed. That is why these strategies require a family systems approach—one characterized by support, collaboration, and intimate interconnectedness. It is imperative to realize that one person cannot do this on their own, and a team effort is vital. If the team does not include family members (e.g., no other family members want to participate), these members can be therapists, physicians, support groups, and other professionals. Likewise, it is also important to have patience, trust, and faith that the process will have a higher likelihood of success, as long as the family stays committed, supportive, and united together.

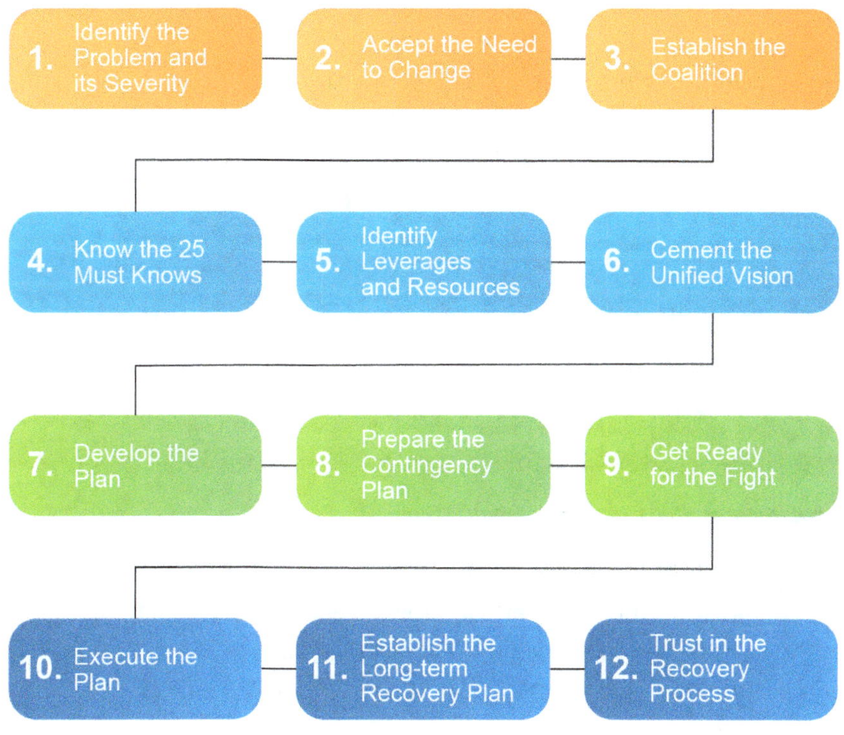

Figure 9. The Step-by-Step Strategic Plan

When I refer to the "primary support system," these are the people intimately involved in information gathering, planning and implementation of the plan. This group has the most influence, is intimately connected to the struggling loved one, and provides the majority of support and resources. The *primary support system* generally includes parents, grandparents, spouses, siblings, later-aged teens (if appropriate) or adult children. The *coalition* is comprised of select persons who will head up the entire process, the decision-makers. Some people in the primary support system may also be in the coalition; however, people in the coalition must be members of the primary support system. The *secondary support system* are people who may not be intimately involved in the information gathering, planning, and implementation of the plan; however, they are an important component of the process, serving to hold boundaries and redirect your loved ones back to the coalition, especially in the early stages of the Pre-treatment Zone and Phases 1-2 of treatment.

Step 1: Identify the problem and its severity.

Why important:

Many times, families are not sure exactly what the problem is, or how severe it really is.

Crucial information to gather at Step 1:

1. Identify the person struggling with the problem (i.e. mental health condition and/or substance abuse disorder).
2. Confirm exactly what the problem is (e.g., family member denying the problem, not taking medications, abusing substances, not caring for basic needs, etc.)
3. Determine what level of crisis the person is in (developing, moderate, imminent). Refer to Chapter 2 for more information on crises.

Important Note: It is essential to consult with a licensed professional (therapist, psychiatrist, medical doctor, social worker, etc.) for further assistance in determining the level of crisis. Several situations warrant being considered a crisis:

- If your loved one is in danger of harming self—has the intent, plans, and means to carry out the act
- Your loved one is in danger of harming others—has the intent, plans, identified victim(s), and means to carry out the act
- Your loved one is gravely disabled—cannot take care of basic needs of food/health/shelter/protection and if their needs are not addressed, there is an extreme, imminent risk for serious harm or death

- It is critical to note that someone in a psychotic state (detached from reality—hallucinations, delusions, disorganized thinking, dissociative state) who meets any of the above criteria is considered to be in crisis.

By using this Step-By-Step plan, it is assumed that your loved one is moving towards an imminent crisis level and other options (i.e., partial hospitalization, intensive outpatient, sober living, outpatient individual/group therapy, AA meetings, community support groups, etc.) have been explored or attempted to no avail and these lower-level options are no longer appropriate based on the family and individual's needs. As you recall, this book is targeted predominantly for those loved ones who need immediate help and treatment to avoid drastic consequences from taking place. At this stage, the family unit typically agrees that detox, inpatient, residential treatment or some other higher levels of care are likely the most fitting interventions at this juncture.

Also, please recall that an imminent crisis means a person needs immediate help; any further delay may entail severe harm to self or others. If your loved one is in imminent crisis, 911 needs to be called immediately.

Establish how long the person has been struggling (e.g., weeks, months, years, decades). In general, struggling for several months (e.g., 1-3 months) at a high degree is reason for concern, but more information is needed to formulate a conclusion or decision.

1. Rate how severe the problem is (Rating Scale: 1—not severe to 10—very severe).
2. Identify potential outcomes if the problem is not addressed (e.g., jail, hospitals, death, harm to others).
3. Identify the people, places, situations, and things perpetuating the problem (e.g., workplace, problematic relationships, unhealthy peer group, substances).

In my work with families, on occasion some family members struggle to recognize exactly what the problem is and the severity of consequences if it's not addressed and resolved. People can be unaware of the reality of the situation due to denial, fear, or lack of knowledge.

It is important for family members to gather as much information as they can and address some of the above questions to fully grasp what is going on with their loved one. Without a true understanding of the circumstances, it will be difficult to attain support from other family members and move forward with a plan.

I suggest you attain a binder, notebook, or folder designated for the research, resources, contact phone numbers, plan, and other information related to getting your struggling family member help. This tool will be the central location for all the essential information needed throughout the process.

Please note: the planning stages may take place over a series of meetings, which is why I suggest you gather the coalition and the primary support system as a first sub-step under the key tasks. However, in some cases with heightened urgency, all critical steps may be addressed in one meeting.

Key Tasks

- Gather together the primary support system.

- Determine if your loved one is in imminent crisis. If so, call 911 immediately for assistance. If not in an imminent crisis but at either developing or moderate levels and may reach imminent crisis level if help is not received soon, proceed with the following recommendations.

- Complete the above sub-steps (Note: The numerical ratings are not to be taken as stand-alone data. The other information mentioned is to be gathered and integrated to supplement the ratings when attempting to make a more comprehensive assessment of the particular issue or situation. Generally speaking, when these scales attain ratings marked with an 8 and above, this rating is significant and indicates a heightened urgency for action and change.)

- Create a central source (e.g., binder, notebook, folder) where all the information regarding the process will be stored and located.

- Document the essential information gathered in this step for future reference.

Step 2: Accept the need to change.

> **Why important:**
>
> Often, families are stuck and fail to recognize the urgency for change. They might think "It will get better," "He will outgrow this," "This is just a phase she's going through because of (insert stressor here)," or, "He will realize he needs to make a change." Acknowledging and accepting the need for change, as well as recognizing the urgency of the matter, are critical at this stage.

Crucial information to gather at Step 2:

Note: Any of the ratings below marked with an 8 and above may indicate a heightened urgency for action or intervention.

1. Rate: How critical is the need for change for the person? (1—not critical to 10—very critical).
2. Rate: How likely is change for the person without support? (1—very likely to 10—very unlikely).
3. Rate: How willing is the person to change? (1—very willing to 10—not willing at all). Recall, people who are unwilling and forced into treatment can be equally successful as people who are willing and motivated. The initial stages of early treatment can provide a level of stabilization whereby a person's levels of willingness and motivation for change can increase as they get healthier.
4. Rate: On average, how committed is the primary support system to making changes? (1—very committed to 10—not committed at all).

5. Identify the barriers to change (e.g., money, lifestyle, peer group, relationship, unwillingness to change, lack of insight into the problem).

6. Identify what efforts have been made by the family system to facilitate change (e.g., confronting the person struggling, offering help, providing resources).

Families need to reach consensus that the problem is an urgent focus and change needs to occur sooner rather than later. I have seen families stagnate and not reach agreement in this step for many reasons—not recognizing how severe the problem is, not knowing what type or level of change needs to take place, not realizing how much power they have in the matter, or not understanding what their role can be in the process for change. Also, fear for their struggling loved one's safety, worry about ramifications to the family unit if an intervention takes place, such as further disconnection of the loved one—all cause families to hesitate to take action. Furthermore, it is vitally important for family members to understand and accept what consequences may occur if changes do not come about. If families have made past attempts to encourage changes, it's crucial to recognize patterns to break the cycle of doing the same thing over and over again and expecting better results (a.k.a "insanity").

Once the family unit recognizes the problem, deems it severe enough to warrant immediate action, and accepts change as necessary to prevent deleterious outcomes, moving on to the next step of assembling the team is appropriate.

Key Tasks

- Gather together the primary support system.

- Complete the above sub-steps (Note: The numerical ratings are not to be taken as stand-alone data. The other information mentioned is to be gathered and integrated to supplement the ratings when attempting to make a more comprehensive assessment of the particular issue or situation. Generally speaking, when these scales attain ratings marked with an 8 and above, this rating is significant and indicates a heightened urgency for action and change.

- Determine if the immediate support system is committed to making the necessary changes.

- Document the essential information gathered in this step for future reference.

Step 3: Establish the coalition.

Why important:

Families need to have a unified front and reach agreement about making the necessary changes. Without a solid vision of what needs to happen, the chances of success are severely impacted.

Crucial information to gather at Step 3:

1. Identify the most essential people needed in the change process (e.g., parents, grandparents, siblings, spouse, relatives, friends) as well as those who will be part of the coalition—people who will be engaged intimately during the entire treatment process.
2. Identify the captain and co-captain. These two individuals will be the heads and main representatives for the primary support system and the coalition, as well as designated as main points of contact. Typically, the captain is the head of the entire process, while the co-captain is the person second in command and serves as a collaborating consultant to the captain. The co-captain will assume the captain role in times when the captain is not able to do so.
3. Identify which person(s) may be problematic or create barriers to your loved ones getting help (e.g., parents, grandparents, siblings, spouse, relatives, friends).
4. Identify the people who may be important parts of the process but need more education, guidance, and convincing (e.g., parents, grandparents, siblings, spouse, relatives, friends).

This step is critical to success. Recall, the coalition is the select team of individuals who will likely be involved throughout the entire recovery process. These people are the key decision-makers, have the most leverage, and provide the resources to get the loved ones help. The coalition should not include people who will not stick through the process in its entirety (more notably in Phases 1 and 2), those resistant to the process, or anyone who may potentially stunt progress in any phase. The coalition should exclude anyone who continues to engage in enabling behaviors. If there are people in the coalition who have struggled with enabling behaviors in the past, they should be vetted to determine whether they can make the necessary changes. It should be determined if they are more helpful or detrimental at this stage of the process.

This is also not the time to worry about hurt feelings or offending anyone. Remember, the top priority is getting your loved ones help, because any further delay can result in tragic consequences. Choose a captain and co-captain to lead the coalition. This is the person or people who will serve as the point of contact and become key decision makers. The captain(s) will organize the treatment process, delegate responsibilities, interface with treatment centers, and create the strategic plan. This person(s) is also the first point of contact. The co-captains work closely with the captains and are people whom the captain trusts to provide sound feedback and insight. Also, co-captains should be entrusted to take the lead if the captains are not able to serve in the role. Furthermore, the captain and co-captain can delegate tasks to other members in the coalition or primary support with whom they trust and when help is needed with responsibilities.

Please note: members of the coalition should be those people who can endure the emotional, mental, and physical distress that may be involved in this stage of the process. They need to think with their hearts and minds, maintaining a balance between the two. If you recall, I call this balance assertive love.

You may encourage the person(s) who struggles with enabling to get help in the form of individual counseling or group support to help navigate through this challenge. Also, a statement to validate his/her importance to the family and communicate his/her value to the unwell loved one but may not be appropriate at this phase of the process are, *"You are an invaluable part of the family, and (name of loved one) needs your support. Perhaps, later on in the process, we can call upon you. It's just that your involvement at this stage of the process may not be a good fit and healthy for both yours and (name of loved one)'s well-being."*

People not included in the coalition may still be involved later in the recovery process. I refer to these helpers as members of either the primary or secondary support systems. They may not be an appropriate or good fit for the early stage of the process, but they are essential to the support network. Also, it's important the coalition is not too large or too small but made up of enough people to support one another and remain cohesive. There is not a magic number for this range. This number can vary depending on factors such as family size, family connectedness, and commitment. However, no matter the size, the people in the coalition need to be emotionally and physically resilient, good communicators, collaborative, assertive, and open-minded but firm (yet flexible when needed) with boundary setting.

Key Tasks

- Gather together the primary support system.

- Determine those people who will serve in the coalition.

- Determine who will serve as the captain and co-captain.

- Begin contacting people in the secondary support system. Contact can be made via email, phone, text, social media, letters, etc. It is up to the family to decide the best approach. It is also up to the family's discretion to determine what information to disclose, and the extent of details given. The main purpose of contacting the secondary support system is to shut down any resources or support the loved one may try to attain from people in the secondary support system.

- Document the essential information gathered in this step for future reference.

Step 4: Know the "25 Must Knows."

Why important:

My "25 Must Knows" encapsulate the essential knowledge I believe is critical before moving on to the next steps. These points address topics such as dealing with guilt, using assertive love, and other strategies to help family members come to the process prepared and well-equipped.

Crucial information to gather at Step 4:

1. Read or re-read (if needed) and understand the "25 Must Knows" in Chapter 4.
2. Focus on Chapter 4, and especially the "Must Knows" involving these specific topics: Releasing Guilt (#4), Enabling (#5), Assertive Love (#6), 3 Inevitable Consequences of Untreated Mental Health and Addiction (#11), Why Desperation is Important (#13), What Leverages Are (#14), What the Non-Negotiables Are (#15), Draining the Battery or Gas Tank (#16), and Validation (#25).

Please note, the "25 Must Knows" are the culmination of my findings from working with hundreds of families. In my experience, the absence of this knowledge has been a barrier to getting struggling family members help.

The "Must Knows" address a wide range of topics on two levels—individual and family. They provide education and strategies for addressing the common barriers for families, as well as factors present when families successfully get their loved ones into treatment.

I can't over-stress the importance of Chapter 4 and the impact it can have on your family's success during this process. Please re-read the chapter if necessary and discuss it with other family members—most especially, everyone in the coalition and primary support system.

Key Tasks

- Gather together the captain, co-captain, coalition, and primary support system.

- Discuss the "25 Must Knows" and ensure a good level of understanding is attained by every member in the primary support system, especially the coalition.

- Reach a consensus or unanimous agreement that everyone in the primary support system and coalition are willing to follow through with the recommendations in the 25 Must Knows as a unified front.

- Continue contacting people in the secondary support system.

- Document the essential information gathered in this step for future reference.

Step 5: Identify leverages and resources

Why important:

As I discussed in the "25 Must Knows," leverages are very important to allow your affected family members to reach a level of desperation, whereby their only options are getting help or entering treatment. Please re-read Chapter 4, Must Know #14: Know to Recognize the Leverage(s), if needed.

Crucial information to gather at Step 5

1. Identify the things, people, places, and situations with the most leverage and capability to put your loved one into a state of desperation (e.g., money, car, place of residence, job, insurance, relationships).

2. Identify how much available money or resources can be committed for the process (e.g., treatment, after-care, sober living).

3. Contact insurance provider (if applicable) to find out the extent of financial coverage (e.g., hospitalizations, detox facility, residential treatment, psychiatric care, psychotherapy, etc.).

4. Research detox facilities (if applicable), hospitals (e.g., mental health behavioral units), treatment facilities/homes (e.g., residential treatment, intensive outpatient, sober livings, etc.). Gather as much information as you can and make a list of contact persons for each place, to be used if or when your loved ones decide to enter treatment. Also, check with insurance providers as to which treatment centers, specific mental health clinicians, or psychiatric providers are covered under the respective coverage plans.

It's imperative to do the groundwork, as not all hospitals, treatment centers, sober livings, programs are created equal. Vet them through online research such as mental health websites (see Chapter 10 for resources), asking acquaintances, consulting with professionals, and calling or visiting the programs, if possible. I highly suggest considering programs that are accredited and licensed, if applicable, to ensure a standard level of care is being met. It is important to note, you cannot leave this research and investigation to your unwell family members in pre-treatment, because they are most likely resistant, unmotivated, unable to think clearly, and not healthy enough to make sound decisions in the vetting process.

Doing the legwork in researching potential treatment programs is a critical step, as many unwell people haven't reached a point of desperation to consider a path to getting help, let alone entering treatment. Remember, those people who have been resistant to help usually have resources or people providing them with capabilities (e.g., money, places to live, transportation, etc.) to continue their current, unhealthy way of living. Please refer to Chapter 4, *Must Knows #13, 14, and 16* for a refresher.

It is also important for families to prepare, as best as possible, for the time when their struggling loved one agrees to seek help. Too many times, when a loved one is faced with choosing between jail or seeking treatment and chooses the latter, the family isn't ready with options, thus missing a vital window of opportunity.

Key Tasks

- Gather together the captain, co-captain, coalition, and primary support system.

- Make a list of the leverages that can be utilized in getting your loved ones to a point of desperation whereby seeking help is their only option.

- Make a list of all resources needed or available to support the treatment process (e.g., finances, insurances).

- Make a list and research potential hospitals, treatment centers or programs your loved ones can enter for treatment.

- Continue contacting people in the secondary support system.

- Document the essential information gathered in this step for future reference.

Step 6: Cement the unified vision

> **Why important:**
>
> Family members need to make sure they are on the same page, with a clear understanding of goals. If not, fractures in the support system may delay the process of unhealthy family members getting help.

Crucial information to gather at Step 6:

1. Confirm that everyone in the coalition has the same vision and is willing to do whatever it takes to stick to the plan.
2. Confirm that the primary support system also supports the vision and is willing to stick to their roles and adhere to the plan.
3. Identify which people will serve as a more critical part of the secondary support system. Though the secondary support system may be large, there may be certain people who are in closer contact and more intimate with the loved one. These are the first people the struggling loved one may contact when firm boundaries are set by the primary support system. The coalition can decide the details of the plan and any further requests to help support the execution of the strategy regarding the secondary support system. Once the strategy is finalized, these identified people should be contacted. The "25 Must Knows" should be discussed with these identified people.

At this step, it should be determined that everyone in the primary support system and coalition is committed to the vision and plan. People can also be identified as critical supports in the secondary support system. This is the juncture at which the family system cannot afford to have people in disagreement, or to regress or alter what was agreed upon. Sometimes, families feel emotional distress, and enabling behaviors result. It's important that everyone clearly understands what the primary goals are, what consequences will result if your loved ones do not get help, and what each person's roles and responsibilities are.

Key Tasks

- Gather together the captain, co-captain, coalition, primary support system, and identified members who are critical in the secondary support system.

- Review what the primary goal is, the importance of everyone sticking to the plan, and the consequences if the struggling family member does not get help.

- Obtain a commitment from everyone in the coalition, primary support system, and identified people in the secondary support system to stick to the goal and plan.

- Continue contacting other essential people in the secondary support system.

- Document the essential information gathered in this step for future reference.

Step 7: Develop the plan

> **Why important:**
>
> It is important to have a very solid plan in place. Everyone should clearly understand their role and who the key players and main point of contacts are. Any holes in the plan will lead to confusion and a potential missed opportunity to get your loved ones help.

Crucial information to gather at Step 7:

1. Determine who, when, and how the boundaries will be set with your unwell family member.
2. Narrow down the list of treatment centers or programs your loved one will enter if or when they agree to treatment.
3. Confirm the resources available to support the costs of the treatment process.
4. Identify the minimum length of time your recovering family members will be in treatment (e.g., 30-45 days, 90 days, 6 months etc.). This does not have to be a set number, as things can change during Phase 1 of treatment. Work collaboratively with the team of professionals gathered (e.g., psychiatrist and/ or therapist of loved one, interventionist, physician, sobriety coach, consultant, social worker, law enforcement, district attorney, judge, etc.) to make a more informed decision on appropriate next steps such as treatment options, level of treatment needed, and to conduct a risk assessment (e.g., suicidality/homicidality, legal ramifications, ability to care for self, etc.).

As mentioned earlier, I suggest a minimum of 45-90 days of

intensive treatment for the best outcomes if your loved one has struggled for a long period of time or has attempted treatment multiple times already, or if the acuity of their mental health or addiction puts them at greater risk of harming themselves or others. I have found it can take a minimum of 30-45 days to even reach a level of adequate baseline stabilization, especially from extremely heightened struggles (e.g., psychotic break, severe manic episode, substance overdose, suicide attempt, nervous breakdown, acute trauma, etc.). From that point forward and once a level of adequate stabilization has been achieved, clients are able to be more stable physically, cognitively, and emotionally to engage in advanced self-introspective or intensive treatment interventions, which is the reason clients struggling at this heightened level are encouraged to be in more intensive treatment up to ninety days minimum.

Confidentiality

Also, when working with the above personnel, it is important to know that your loved one's therapists, psychiatrists, or doctors are legally bound to adhere to privacy rules (confidentiality) and cannot speak about the case without consent. This restriction of what providers can disclose to family members can be stressful and frustrating, especially when loved ones are in crisis. However, limits to confidentiality include any suspicion of potential or imminent suicidal or homicidal ideation (i.e., intent, plan, means, and identified target (for homicidality), child or elderly abuse or neglect, or when immediate and imminent medical help is needed. In these instances, Emergency Medical Services (EMS) and/or law enforcement must be contacted by the clinician or other professional via mandatory reporting statutes. This limit to confidentiality may or may not include family members (assuming an adult client) and may vary across states or counties.

Identify any weak areas, loopholes, or potential breaches in the plan (e.g., people who may enable, resources your loved ones may tap into such as money, friends, housing, or legal issues such as the timeline for the rightful execution of an eviction notice).

Many times, family members do not have a solid plan in place. They are unsure about their roles and responsibilities or what to do if their loved one decides they need care and treatment. Finances have not been set up to fund treatment, or there is no decision about the strategy if unwell family members decide to abandon the recovery process. Of course, not every scenario can be prepared for, but it's important to try to cover as many bases as possible. In Step 9, I will discuss what to say when setting boundaries, and steps to take when requesting your loved one get help.

Key Tasks

- Gather together the captain, co-captain, coalition, primary support system, and identified members who are critical in the secondary support system.

- Draft a solidified plan from the information gathered above. (Helpful tip: The plan answers the questions *who, what, when, where, and how.*)

- *Who* – The person(s) critical to developing the plan. They will communicate the plan to your loved one and serve as key points of contact at treatment facilities and other involved entities, etc.

- *What* - What are the treatment options if the loved one agrees to the plan, what are the plans if the loved one continues to refuse help/treatment, and what are the boundaries or non-negotiables the family agrees to uphold, etc.

- *When* – The timeframe within which the loved one needs to agree to get help, any deadlines established to comply with any boundaries, which day the family agrees to send loved one to treatment, dates when a bed is available at a selected treatment facility, etc.

- *Where* - The location where the plan will be communicated to your loved one, location of treatment facility, etc.

- *How* – By what means will the plan be communicated to your loved one, how will boundaries be presented, and the method of transportation to take the loved one to the treatment facility, etc.

- Review what the primary goal is, the importance of everyone sticking to the plan, and the consequences if the struggling family member does not get help.

- Contact those people who may be major barriers to the plan (e.g., critical people in the secondary support system, enablers) and educate them on the importance of your loved ones getting help.

- Continue contacting people who are essential in the secondary support system.

- Document the essential information gathered in this step for future reference.

Step 8: Prepare the contingency plan

> **Why important:**
>
> Families need to be ready in case the plan does not go as they hoped. It is important to have alternative options for when the situation does not proceed as planned.

Crucial information to gather at Step 8:

1. Decide on plans if your loved ones do not accept your offer for help or treatment.
2. If your unwell family members enter treatment, decide what to do if they want to leave treatment prematurely, or leave against medical advice.
3. Your plan of action should include contacting people in the primary and secondary support systems to advise what to do if your loved one abandons the plan prematurely and begins contacting other family members for support. Suggest these family members hold boundaries and redirect your loved ones back to the coalition, more specifically the captain and co-captain. Refer to the "Must Knows" in Chapter 4 as needed.

Often, families new to the treatment process are not prepared when affected family members take flight (run away) or leave treatment prematurely. Fear and emotions can take over and families could abandon the plan. It is critical for family members to accept the 3 Inevitable Consequences of Untreated Mental Health and Addiction (See Chapter 4, *Must Know #10 and 11*). Family members must stay firm with their boundaries and stick to the plan. The disease does not want to cooperate and wishes to take flight. The family's job is to anticipate this and continue limiting options. This boundary setting will push the loved one to a point of desperation, where returning for help is the only way to attain support.

Key Tasks

- Gather together the captain, co-captain, coalition, primary support system, and identified members who are critical in the secondary support system.

- Review what the primary goal is, the importance of everyone sticking to the plan, and the consequences if the struggling family member does not get help.

- Obtain a commitment from everyone in the coalition and primary support system to stick to the goal and plan.

- Confirm the contingency plans for when your unwell family members refuse help or leave treatment prematurely. Be sure to tell people in the primary and secondary support systems whom to direct your unwell family members to if they reach out. This is usually the captain and co-captain.

- Continue contacting essential people in the secondary support system.

- Document the essential information gathered in this step for future reference.

Step 9: Get ready for the fight

Why important:

Sometimes family members get cold feet. Fear sets in and the plan starts to fray. It's very important to support one another and reiterate the primary goal—getting your untreated family members help.

Crucial information to gather at Step 9:

1. Solidify the plan using the information gathered in Steps 1-8.
2. Confirm that everyone in the coalition, primary and secondary support systems are still committed to the plan, goals, and decided methods to get your loved ones help.
3. Identify everyone as best as possible in the secondary support system, letting them know the situation and what you are requesting of them. The people in the secondary support system do not need to know intimate details about the struggles your unwell family members are experiencing. This is up to the families' discretion. You can talk to the secondary support system personally, or send an email, message, or text informing them. A general message without revealing intimate details can sound something like, "If (name of your loved one) contacts you, we can really use your support and kindly redirect him/her back to (point of contact). They are going through some challenges at the current time and can really use your help. Feel free to contact (point of contact) if you have any questions. Thank you."
4. Confirm the plan, in the case of your struggling family member becoming aggressive (e.g., making threatening comments, gestures, or behaviors), or posing an imminent danger to self

or others, requiring that the police be called. Please refer to Chapter 4, *Must Know #18* for examples of language to use when contacting law enforcement.

5. Discuss and rehearse "What If" cases and the plan of action to address these scenarios. Some examples of What Ifs are: Your unwell family members show up at your home unexpectedly, try to break in, then use threatening language or behaviors toward family members. Or the family gets a call from the hospital, police, boss, co-worker, friend, etc. Try to address as many scenarios as possible. Again, no one can ever be overly prepared, but families can definitely be underprepared.

In intense situations involving a confrontation, argument, conflict resolution, competition, or fight—emotions, thoughts, and behaviors are intermixed at a heightened stress level. One of the most effective ways to manage these stressful reactions and maximize outcomes is to be prepared. You can never fully cover all possible scenarios to reduce stress, but you can work hard to plan and create a foundation that is adaptive across many situations.

I mentioned earlier that fear and anxiety—as well as other emotions—can be beneficial, especially at low-to-moderate levels and may even serve as a source of motivation. But when these emotions are at high levels for long periods of time, they can become destabilizing and paralyzing. Please recognize that all levels of emotions are likely throughout this process, most especially in the Pre-treatment Zone through Phase 2 (e.g., anxiety, guilt, fear, worry, sadness, anger, etc.). Confusion, guilt, and uncertainty are valid and legitimate emotions, but high levels of these emotions in these early phases may prevent the plan from solidifying, or reflect that certain people are not fully onboard with executing the strategies. Consequently, these unmanaged emotions can impair decision-making and fracture the unity needed between all critical members of the support system. Based on my experience, these emotions will lessen as your recovering family member gets better over time. I have seen anxiety, fear, and desperation evolve into relief, courage, and hope as the loved one gets healthier.

It is critical that everyone in the primary support system and coalition are working on one hundred percent of their share of accountability. This share of responsibility includes managing one's own self-care. With that said, seeking your own therapy, support groups, spiritual guidance, life coaching, etc. are important to help manage these emotions and other challenges that may present as barriers to executing the plan (e.g., co-dependent relationships, enabling behaviors, unresolved grief and loss, struggles with sobriety, unprocessed guilt, etc.).

Key Tasks

- Gather together the captain, co-captain, coalition, primary support system, and identified members who are critical in the secondary support system.

- Discuss and rehearse the "What If" scenarios.

- Discuss and finalize a plan in case law enforcement is needed for intervention. Please read Chapter 4, *Must Know #18* for information about making a call to law enforcement.

- Review Chapters 3, Understanding the Disease, and Chapter 5, the 80-20 model. Make a plan for shutting down the twenty percent (the disease's manipulation aspect).

- Review what the primary goal is, the importance of everyone sticking to the plan, and the consequences if the struggling family member does not get help.

- Obtain a commitment from everyone in the coalition and primary and secondary support systems to stick to the goal and plan.

- Confirm the contingency plans for when your unwell family members refuse help or leave treatment prematurely. Be sure to tell people in the primary and secondary support systems whom should be contacted if your unwell family members reach out. This is usually the captain and co-captain.

- Continue contacting essential people in the secondary support system.

- Document the essential information gathered in this step for future reference.

Step 10: Execute the plan

Why important:

Families can have the best plans in place, but those plans become meaningless without effective execution. Executing the plan may be the most difficult step but will produce dramatic life changes for your suffering family member.

Crucial information to gather at Step 10:

1. Decide when you will communicate the plan to your unwell family members, and who will deliver the message. If they are in jail or the behavioral unit of a hospital, this is an opportune time to let them know they cannot return home or receive your support if they do not follow through with the proposed treatment plan. These are optimal locations to communicate this information to your loved ones because if they act out in

anger or attempt to harm themselves or others, they will be in a controlled setting with support services to provide the appropriate care and supervision. If your loved one is homeless, be careful and mindful and take safety measures into account. Some factors to be diligent in considering are environmental conditions (abandoned buildings, isolated areas out of the public eye, the presence of dangerous items such as needles and contraband, weapons your loved one may have to protect self while homeless, etc.) and other people in the surrounding area who may be mentally unstable or pose a potential threat.

    a. The family has a lot of leverage at this point, because the loved one may find themselves with only one option, treatment. As a safety precaution, at least two people should be present when setting the boundary for support. Also, having a team during this time also lets your loved ones know the plan is not coming from one person, but rather, from a group of caring individuals.

    b. *Note*: Some families may choose to hire a professional interventionist to assist or head-up this process. A discussion with the family support system should take place to discuss this option and its appropriateness thoroughly.

2. Be mindful of safety factors when setting the boundary. Safety for all parties involved is of primary importance, and diligent planning is needed. For instance, you do not want to bring up the plan if your unwell family members are under the influence, highly agitated, belligerent, or highly distressed (i.e., in a panic attack, suicidal, extremely depressed, expressing aggressive behaviors, in a psychotic episode, or with access to weapons). Sometimes a public venue or somewhere outside the home may be an appropriate place to have the discussion. Family members should use their best judgment.

a. Utilize a 3-Step boundary setting method. Unless your untreated family members are in imminent danger to themselves or others (which would require assistance from law enforcement and a psychological assessment), I suggest a 3 Try Approach. Any time a boundary needs to be set with anyone (e.g., with a child, co-worker, friend, spouse, romantic partner, etc.), I recommend three tries before taking the action steps discussed up to this point.

    i. **1st Attempt**: Calm and open dialogue about what you are asking of your unwell family members. *"We are concerned about you and want to help. We feel that getting some help with your struggles is very important for your well-being. Can we discuss our concerns, what you feel you are struggling with, what we can do to help, what you feel you need to get better, and come up with a plan together? We care about you and want to help."*

    ii. **2nd Attempt:** More assertive, reiterating the concern, expressing the importance of getting help, and relaying the plan the family has in place. Please note: being assertive in this situation does not mean to use a loud, screaming volume or an "in your face" demeanor, which will come off as aggressive and heighten defensiveness in your loved one. Rather, a calm but firm voice and presentation are key to being assertive. Ironically, some of the most assertive people I have come across have been shorter in stature and smaller in size but convey a serious and confident tone when speaking. The family should determine a reasonable timeframe for when this 2nd attempt should take place after making the 1st attempt (e.g., a few days, 1-2 weeks, a month, etc.). Be cognizant of the micro changes that may be taking place, because due to chronic fear and desperation, families may not recognize actual progress is occurring with their loved ones and may need to reassess and revise the plan. The family will have to use their best discretion in deciding what action steps need to be taken based on the acuity of your loved ones and their exposure to risk. An example of dialogue during the second attempt may sound like, *"We have discussed our concerns already, and we are still worried about your struggles and your well-being. We need you to decide about your plans to address the goals we set out for you. We cannot continue to support you, and you will not be able to stay here if you do not seek help. We are letting you know what the options are. We are here to assist you. Please decide whether you will be adhering to our requests. We hope you decide to accept our help, and know we care for you."*

iii. **3ʳᵈ Attempt:** Assertive tone and language, letting them know this is the last opportunity to get help. Again, reiterate the concern, express the importance of getting help, and relay the plan the family has in place. The family should determine a reasonable timeframe within which this 3ʳᵈ attempt should take place after making the 2ⁿᵈ attempt (e.g., a few days, 1-2 weeks, a month, etc.)—this time, it should be a shorter span of time. The family should use their best discretion in deciding what action steps need to be taken based on the acuity of your loved ones and exposure to risk. An example of dialogue for the 3ʳᵈ attempt is, *"We have tried our best to give you enough time to decide how you would like to proceed in getting help, and we are very concerned for your well-being. This is the last time we will speak on this topic. If you do not decide by (give a* *timeframe, a few days maximum) this time, you can no longer stay here, and we will no longer support you."*

    b. <u>Note</u>: Many city or state laws indicate at least a thirty-day notice prior to eviction of your adult loved ones if they receive mail at the residence, pay for rent, or have resided at the residence for a period of time. Please check local laws regarding evictions.

    c. If you strongly suspect your loved one may not adhere to the plan, it may be best to commence the eviction process earlier rather than waiting until after the 3rd attempt, which will consequently allow your loved one an extra 30-60 days to reside in the home. If the eviction process is started earlier (before or during 1st or 2nd attempt), they will have only days or a week to leave the premises. In the best-case scenario, your loved one agrees to the plan, and the eviction notice may be rescinded or terminated.

    d. If or when your adult loved ones are no longer under your care and they are still refusing help, the process of setting them up to a point of desperation commences. Please review Chapter 4, *Must Knows 4, 6, 10, 12, 13, 15, 16, 17, 19, and 20*. Also remember to keep planting the emotional seeds during this time as discussed in Chapter 4, Must Know #19.

Step 10, the execution of the plan, is probably the most distressful, unsettling, and fearful part of the process. But it's also, perhaps, the most important one. Stay strong and take care of one another and yourselves. It's critically important to trust in the process. As long as everyone is doing their part, taking accountability, understanding their roles, and holding to the non-negotiables, the chances of success during this step are greatly increased.

Key Tasks

- Gather together the captain, co-captain, coalition, primary support system, and identified members who are critical in the secondary support system.

- Discuss and finalize a plan in case law enforcement is needed.

- Make sure the treatment options are solidified for if or when your loved ones are ready to enter treatment.

- Continue to discuss and rehearse the "What If" scenarios.

- Review Chapters 5, 6, 7, and 9 to get an overall view of the recovery process and the factors needed to be successful in the long-term.

- Continue contacting essential people in the secondary support system.

- Document the essential information gathered in this step for future reference.

Step 11: Establish a long-term recovery plan

Why important:

Many times, families see treatment as the final stage, not realizing recovery is a life-long process. Families need to acknowledge the process may look a little different as time progresses and as their loved one gets healthier, but recovery is the most important goal for everyone.

Crucial information to gather at Step 11:

1. Determine what Phase 2 and 3 are going to entail (e.g. full or part-time job, daily AA meetings, weekly or biweekly individual therapy sessions, monthly psychiatric visits, etc.). Make it a collaborative effort, including your loved ones and treatment team (if available) as they are in a healthier place and can begin taking ownership over their recovery program.

2. Review Chapter 4, Must Knows 3, 15, 24, 25 and Chapter 5 (The Disease Vaccine—H2O) to help understand the factors needed for your loved ones to be successful in the long-term, what to expect in the process, and how the family unit can continue to support the recovery journey.

3. Review Chapter 7 on the Phases of Recovery to get an overall view of the recovery process.

4. Confirm with your recovering family members, the family unit, and the treatment team what recovery will look like in Phases 2 and 3.

5. Ensure resources are available (e.g., finances and insurance) to cover the cost of after-care treatment (Phases 2-3).

6. Confirm with the coalition and primary and secondary support systems that everyone will stand firm with the non-negotiables moving forward.

At this stage, there can be a mix of emotions. Hopefully, by Phases 2-3, there is less fear, hopelessness, and concern for all involved. If your recovering family members are working with a stronger recovery program, they may begin to have hope, feel better, and have more optimism about making changes in their lives. The family unit also can begin feeling more comfortable in their roles during the recovery process, and grateful their loved ones are getting better. Family members may also begin reconnecting with other people in their lives (e.g., kids, grandkids, spouses), and focusing more on their own self-care.

Congratulations for making it this far! It was not an individual effort, but a team-oriented one that took patience, love, fight, hope, and resilience. As I mentioned earlier, recovery will be the most important aspect for your loved ones and your family from here on out because, without it, nothing else is possible nor able to reach its best potential. Recovery will always need to be attended to, prioritized, adaptive, and improved each and every day.

Key Tasks

- Gather together the captain, co-captain, coalition, primary support system, and identified members who are critical in the secondary support system.

- Collaborate with your loved ones, the family, and treatment team on what treatment will look like in Phases 2-3.

- Continue to discuss and rehearse the "What If" scenarios.

- Continue to review Chapters 5, 6, 7, and 9 to get an overall view of the recovery process and the factors to be successful in the long-term.

- Continue contacting essential people in the secondary support system.

- Document the essential information gathered in this step for future reference.

Step 12: Trust in the recovery process

> **Why important:**
>
> Family members sometimes become mentally stuck, waiting for the "next shoe to drop" and failing to allow the process to proceed with its course. As long as everyone is doing their part, family members can trust that things will work out in the way they are supposed to, and all answers will come through recovery.

Crucial information to gather at Step 12:

1. Determine what Phase 4 will involve. This conversation can involve your loved ones, or, if they are in a better place and have a strong recovery program solidified, they can take full ownership.
2. Determine with the family support system what your roles will be at this juncture of the recovery process.

An even bigger congratulations to everyone! It's okay to be proud of yourselves for making it this far! At this point, your loved ones are looking and feeling much better. They may be taking on much higher-level goals such as attending college, enrolling into graduate school, narrowing down a career path, working full-time, starting their own business, having a serious relationship, getting married, or even planning to have children. The family unit is now at a point to start re-focusing on their own lives. The hope is much stronger that recovery may be potentially long-term.

It will always be important for your loved ones to respect the capabilities of their disease, as family members recognize and continue to work on their own respective diseases. If everyone maintains a strong recovery program, the family can have unlimited potential, with the capabilities to manage whatever life drops in their path.

Key Tasks

- Gather together the captain, co-captain, coalition, primary support system, and identified members who are critical in the secondary support system (if necessary).

- Collaborate with your loved ones and the family on what treatment will look like in Phase 4 (if they need the collaboration).

- Always maintain a high degree of H20 for everyone in the family.

- Maintain all documents in a binder or folder, in case problems should arise again.

- Continue to have open communication and support one another.

- Move forward with your lives, achieve your goals, and trust in the recovery process.

- Document the key points of information gathered.

This step-by-step procedure is designed to help families establish a unified vision and help construct an action plan. I coach families but try–when possible—to defer to them as the experts in ultimately deciding what is best for the family, most especially when they are working collaboratively and with the healthiest mindset possible. That said, I encourage families to tailor, revise, and amend these steps in a fashion that is most befitting for their family based on their needs, resources, and beliefs. These steps are to be used as an educational tool and guide in solidifying the final strategic plan.

Chapter 9
The Path to Lifelong Recovery

This chapter is designed to discuss some of the common questions that come up during the early recovery process and to offer some answers that may improve the chances for long-term success. I will discuss decision-making and relationships in recovery, the importance of prioritizing recovery, how time in recovery relates to long-term success, jobs/careers/volunteer work/school in early recovery, rebuilding trust with your loved one, and the factors most consistently observed in families with successful, long-term results. This chapter will provide a motivating preview of what early recovery can look like.

Remember, recovery is a life-long process for everyone who was involved with treatment and continues to be a part of the journey. It's a process that requires regular attention and constantly evolving needs; consistent adaptation to life circumstances is key. Life is always changing, and we can never know what nature will put in our path. Even in the most harrowing of situations, completely unexpected circumstances, or the most severe of traumatic events, many people have affirmed, with gratitude, that their recovery program helped them through those turbulent storms.

In my work with hundreds of families and clients who continue to remain successful, one constant, across the board, is that recovery remains the most important aspect of their lives. They know without it, nothing else is fully possible, and they can't reach the best version of themselves (e.g., being a responsible parent, loving spouse, dependable friend, diligent employee, etc.). Often, some of the most fulfilling, happiest, and satisfying memories people recall are the experiences they had in recovery.

Decision-making and relationships in recovery

I tell clients and family members that all decisions and answers emanate from a healthy recovery program. In fact, life solutions regarding family relationships, friendships, romantic connections, career opportunities, job promotions, and other critical decisions in their lives are embedded in their recovery. Whenever clients are at an impasse with a decision, I ask, "What does your recovery tell you?" Remember, recovery includes fellowship (e.g., therapists, healthy peers, family), acquired knowledge, a clearer conscience, H20, etc. I advise them to consider their fellowship in decision-making and ask, "What would they recommend I do?" This type of pretend inquiry (in case they are not able to ask directly) serves as sort of a jury for making conscientious and more informed decisions.

For instance, if a young adult male is contemplating dating a female who is only three weeks sober and is experiencing a lot of personal issues, he should ask himself, "How is this relationship going to impact my recovery?" Another example could be a female trying to decide whether to apply for a job that would cause her a great deal of stress due to the travel requirements and numerous fast-paced deadlines each month. She would ask, "How will this job impact my recovery?" In both instances, if these situations will not have a positive impact on recovery, the decision should reflect that these situations are not a good fit at that moment in time. It's not a judgment on the person or the job; it merely means they are not a good idea for the person and their recovery. This same concept extends to family members, relatives, and good friends. The reality is, some people within an interpersonal circle may not be healthy for your loved ones' recovery (e.g., a parent who is not sober, a sibling who is verbally abusive, a cousin who engages in illegal activities, or a good friend who is being reckless with his/her life). In cases like these, your loved ones need to set healthy boundaries and protect their recovery. Again, it is not a judgment on anyone. Your loved ones need to realize which relationships or situations are appropriate in their lives to maintain a strong recovery.

If clients have people in their lives who are not supportive of their recovery, they should decide whether they can afford to keep them in their sphere of support. Sometimes, certain people or situations are not a good fit due to the phase of recovery your loved ones are in (e.g., getting together for dinner with a friend who drinks on occasion, a cousin who is depressed and not getting help, going on a vacation that may create emotional triggers, etc.). Further down the road, those same people, places, or situations can either become healthier, or your loved ones will develop a much stronger recovery program to navigate through these types of stressful situations more effectively. In those circumstances, certain people or situations can be reintroduced back into their lives.

By approaching these difficult decisions from a relationship level rather than an individual level, your loved ones will be able to mini-mize the emotional aspect and view their decisions more clearly. One case example reflecting this idea was a client who was three months sober and dating a woman who was still abusing alcohol. He knew that her drinking was a problem putting his recovery at risk, but he felt guilty because she had stuck by him in the past, helping him through some rough periods. The girlfriend had no plans to give up her drinking any time soon, and he didn't know what to do. I advised him to look at the situation from a relationship level and not an individual one. "How is this relationship impacting your recovery/sobriety?" The answer immediately crystallized. Looking at the situation through the relationship lens removed the guilt component when he viewed it from the individual (e.g., girlfriend) level. He knew her drinking was putting his recovery at risk. He was grateful for what she had done for him and acknowledged they may reconnect again in the future if she decided to get healthy. He also realized he would be doing her more harm than good by staying, thereby giving her a green light that he approved of her drinking. He did not want to co-sign her unhealthy narrative. The next time I saw him, he had spoken to her. She said she understood, and their discussion had encouraged her to think about her own sobriety.

One last strategy I share with clients, especially in early recovery, is asking them to look at their phone and observe the last thirty or so people they were in contact with (e.g., text, call, social media, etc.), prior to treatment. I instruct them to decipher which of those people are unhealthy for their recovery. From there, they can decide if some relationships need boundaries, or if some should be removed from their contact list, altogether. These latter people can be drug dealers, toxic relationships, or people who have no desire to get healthy and pose a great risk to the loved one's recovery. Some clients, prior to discharge from treatment, work with therapists or case managers to scour their phones and laptops, deleting contacts, social media sites, messages, emails, or texts that cause a great deal of distress or will do more harm than good to their recovery. All these elements can negatively impact a new, healthy lifestyle.

Recovery—The center point of healthy living

Recovery needs to be at the center of clients' lives to maximize their chances for long-term success. It should be the cornerstone of physical, mental, and social health, while everything else becomes secondary. That is not to say that these secondary aspects are less important, it merely signifies they are meaningless without recovery. Without recovery, nothing else is possible from a health standpoint. Family members need to realize and accept this new lifestyle and understand when loved ones cannot get together because they have a sobriety meeting to attend, a group therapy session scheduled, or an appointment with a sobriety sponsor to work on recovery steps.

To illustrate these points, I use the image of a dartboard when working with clients and family members to show how recovery needs to be at the center of importance.

Figure 10 shows recovery/sobriety at the bullseye (center) of your recovering loved ones' lives. Everything else comes secondary to it, because the secondary factors are severely compromised if they veer from recovery. When your loved one keeps recovery as a central aspect of daily life, they dramatically increase their chances for long-term success.

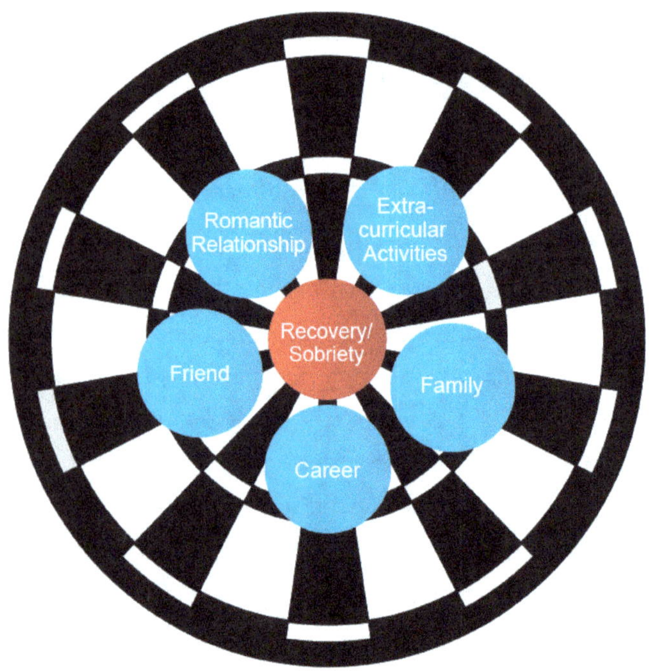

Figure 10. Dartboard of Recovery Priority—Center of Importance

Conversely, Figure 11 shows the typical pattern when people start to struggle, relapse, or lapse. When recovery is no longer at the core of their lives, becoming secondary and moving to the outskirts of priority, something else will often take its place (e.g., career, family, friends, etc.).

It's worth noting that new romantic relationships in Phase 1 and Phase 2 of recovery are highly discouraged from a treatment standpoint. In my work with clients, a new romantic relationship within the first thirty-to-ninety days of treatment invariably (about ninety percent of the time) leads to a relapse or lapse, especially if the new love interest does not have a recovery program in place or support the client's recovery. Clients in Phase 1 and 2 of treatment are emotionally vulnerable, working on their traumas, navigating through PAWS, attaining new coping skills, and working on breaking old patterns. Being involved in a new relationship can pull them away from recovery, making it secondary in importance. Typically, it's recommended to wait a minimum of six months—but preferably a year at minimum—prior to starting a new relationship. Granted, some clients are already in relationships or marriages before treatment and in those circumstances, relationships need to receive diligent attention—perhaps via couple's therapy, while still keeping recovery first and foremost.

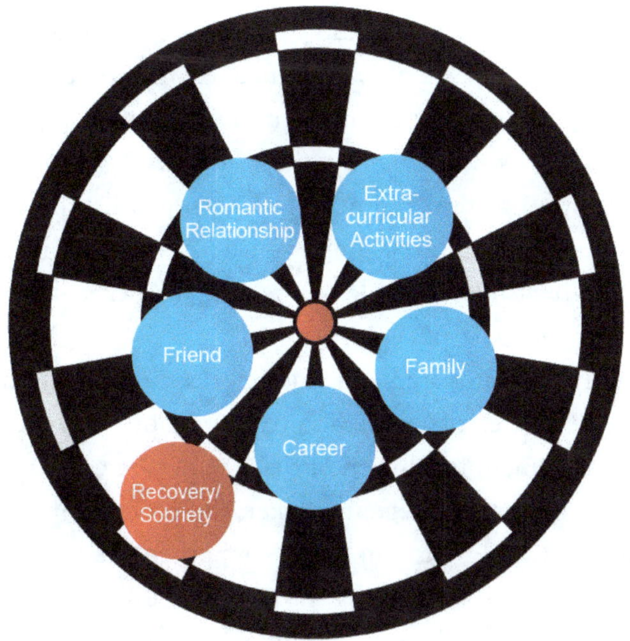

Figure 11. Dartboard of Recovery Priority—Secondary in Importance

Time in recovery and probability of long-term success

Consistently, I find a correlation between time spent in recovery and increased probability of long-term success. Remember, treatment doesn't cure people, per se, but maximizes their chances of success by attaining a level of stabilization, providing healthier options, establishing healthy habits and routines, and previewing what a healthy lifestyle can look like. Legendary football coach Vince Lombardi once said, "The harder you work, the harder it is to surrender." When someone puts in the hard work to accomplish something, the more they will fight to protect it. Examples of rejecting the option of surrender can be a couple working diligently on their long-term marriage, a person arduously climbing the corporate ladder at a job, or a valued, long-lasting friendship surviving its share of trials and tribulations.

This same idea relates to recovery and sobriety. Someone with one year of sobriety under their belt is more likely to be protective and avoid risky behaviors that can lead to relapse, compared to someone with only one day of sobriety. Even someone with twenty-four days of sobriety will have more fight compared to someone with just twenty-four hours. That is, the time invested in recovery or sobriety can have a correlation to the level of fight a person will summon not to sabotage it. For this reason, keeping your recovering family members in step-down treatment for at least one year skyrockets their chances for long-term success.

However, time invested does not necessarily equal success. A person can be in treatment for one year and not be as successful as someone in treatment for three months. The person with shorter time may have worked more diligently, taken the process more seriously, and acted as a willing participant to strengthen their recovery program. Of course, this is assuming the two people are similar in acuity levels, diagnoses, struggles, and family supports, because individual differences may lead to one person needing more time to get better than another. Actor Denzel Washington told a university graduating class, "Just because you are doing a lot, does not mean you are getting a lot done." Similarly, when people falsely think that time spent invariably leads to progress and success, I tell them, "You can run around for three hours in circles and not get anywhere." Progress requires intentional and directional movement and time spent moving aimlessly is counterproductive. In terms of my phase models (Phases 1-4), there is an assumption that the loved one—and, at minimum, the primary family support system—will be active and engaged participants during the treatment process if a successful recovery program is to be established. Indeed, some clients opt not to have any family support in place during the early recovery process, due to estrangement or toxicity in their relationship dynamics. These clients attempt to navigate through Phases 1 and 2 virtually solo. They may have resources (i.e., finances, place to live, job, etc.) to carry on independently without support—which means there is little to no leverage over them. It's not impossible to be successful without a network of support during the early points in recovery, but the probability of long-term success is greatly lessened without it, as fellowship is critical for a strong recovery program. If the support network won't involve family members, it's vital that clients create a support system of other people to surround their recovery (e.g., sobriety peers and healthy friends).

Jobs/volunteering/school in early recovery

Clients and family members often ask me where jobs, volunteer work, and attending school fit into the recovery process. These areas are common and important components of treatment/recovery, because the majority of adult clients I've observed in residential treatment range between 18-40 years of age and are still working age. I estimate that eighty-five percent of clients have reached a level of readiness for a job, school, or volunteer work once they enter Phase 2 of treatment. However, there is a percentage of clients (around fifteen percent or so) who need more time in treatment before these activities will be appropriate (they may have heightened PAWS, still be psychotic, or need further stabilization). These clients may need to wait longer to reach a healthier baseline. A job, school, or volunteer work can provide a level of structure, routine, and accountability that might greatly benefit treatment. Clients should explore and discuss these activities in conjunction with family and the treatment team to determine what is best for their recovery.

When clients decide it's appropriate to find a job in recovery, the first one is commonly referred to as a "get well job." This does not have to be the client's long-term career or the perfect fit for their aspirations. This first job is intended to assist a smooth transition back into community life. It should be one that's not too stressful and will support their recovery program. Some of the recommended elements for a first job following Phase 1 are a physical location to report to (e.g., office, facility, center), a clear, designated supervisor or manager, job tasks and responsibilities that are clearly defined, and pay that occurs in equal intervals (e.g., every two weeks, every month). Jobs that require clients to be alone or isolated, with no one to report to, unclear responsibilities, or irregular paychecks are not recommended, as they compromise structure, routine, and accountability. Of course, jobs like growing marijuana, working as a bartender, organizing rave concerts, or graveyard/late night shifts (e.g., lone security guard at a site), or others that increase the risk curve are not conducive to early recovery, if ever.

Attending school may seem like a great idea, but overall, it's not always feasible, especially during early recovery. Sometimes, family members believe school and academic goals are a positive component in a recovery program and, in some instances, they feel it's critically important for their loved ones to immediately return to achieving their educational pursuits. But, I have seen clients struggle while attending college, especially if their days are not structured. They can attend one class in the morning and have a five-hour break before the next class. With that much time, boredom can set in—which can be detrimental for recovery. Some clients have decided to take on a full-time school load (twelve units or more) in early recovery, then became too distressed and ended up dropping out, which lowered self-esteem and hopefulness. I usually recommend clients take one to two classes when in Phase 2 and diligently increase their class load over time as they proceed in recovery. The clients can also work closely with their school counselor to outline a class schedule that befits a strong recovery path.

Again, families, clients and the treatment team should decide what is best, as all clients' needs, strengths, and recovery programs vary.

Rebuilding trust

According to *Oxford English Dictionary, trust* is the "firm belief in the reliability, truth, ability, or strength of someone or something." Trust is one of the most concerning topics that consistently arises on both client ("When will my family trust me again?") and family levels ("When can we trust him/her again?"). In fact, whenever I am helping clients identify their protective factors in recovery, I ask for the reasons why they are choosing to get healthy, stay in treatment, or avoid relapse and lapse. The most common answer involves wanting to gain trust from their family members again. The most re-occurring concern families express is whether they can open up again and trust their loved ones.

The answer to both questions is simple: *Truth over time builds trust.* This statement has been one of the most powerful communicated to me in my clinical work by a private practice client, who I will refer to as "Kelly." These words have had a profound impact whenever I am helping clients and family members find peace with the trust process.

To illustrate this notion more clearly, let me share some of Kelly's background information. She was a grandmother who struggled with alcohol for decades since her daughter was a child. Kelly suffered countless relapses throughout her daughter's life, severely fracturing trust. The longest span of abstinence she ever attained was two years. Kelly's adult daughter eventually had a baby girl and decided to set a boundary with Kelly: "Until you get sober for at least a good amount of time (didn't give a timeframe), I can't have you in my or my daughter's lives." Kelly was understandably distraught but deep down knew the boundary was appropriate. In her search for answers on how to rebuild trust with her daughter, a dear friend of hers who was involved in AA and had years of sobriety relayed those words, "Truth over time builds trust."

I advised Kelly to stop trying to convince her daughter of how trustworthy she was (constant reminders she was going to AA meetings, attending therapy sessions, successful accounting of days of not drinking, etc.). Whenever someone goes out of their way to prove trustworthiness, that person is going about it the wrong way—attaining trust should be a natural process. In other words, people should be able to trust someone based on factors such as the content of their speech (authenticity, honesty), the energy they emit (humility, optimism, positivity, hopefulness), and the consistency of their actions (words reflecting behaviors, doing what they say they are going to do, being open to feedback). It then dawned on me that these attributes are all outcomes of a strong sobriety/recovery plan. I told Kelly if she could focus and have faith in her recovery program, trust would begin to manifest, and her daughter would eventually trust again. As long as she stayed true to her word, in time, a foundation of trust would be built.

After one year of sobriety, Kelly was back in her daughter's life and met her granddaughter for the first time. Kelly's daughter could tell her mom was in a healthy place based on her language clarity, calm demeanor, manicured look, and spiritual energy. She found an authenticity; in the past, Kelly did not exhibit trustworthiness and lied about her abstinence. Essentially, true sobriety/recovery cannot be fabricated, and the person's presentation is not convincing—especially to their most intimate family members—when they are not healthy.

Based on Kelly's success with her daughter, *Truth over time builds trust* has been the most convincing message I tell clients worried about earning their family members' confidence. I advise them not to prove how trustable they are; a strong recovery program will invariably and eventually build trust—a byproduct gift of sobriety/recovery. This notion has worked for people who have sabotaged trust for years and decades. Family members, for the most part, want to trust again.

When family members do their parts (set healthy boundaries, focus on their own recovery, and work 100% on their accountability), trust will likely come back again—provided their loved one stays in recovery.

Factors consistent with long-term success

Below are the factors I most consistently recognize associated with long-term recovery. They are factors present in both clients and families who achieved success throughout the process. With the exception of the last three bullet points below, all of these factors were discussed thoroughly in the book, so I will not expand upon them again here. I have provided the chapters to find these concepts in case you need a review.

The elements or behaviors commonly present in those with a strong recovery program:

- <u>Honesty</u>, <u>Humility</u>, <u>Openness to Direction</u>—H20 (Chapter 5)
- Structure, routine, accountability (Chapter 7)
- Flattened risk curve (Chapter 6)
- Family assuming equal responsibility (Chapter 4, *Must Know #7*)
- Supporting only the recovery narrative (Chapter 4, *Must Know #3*)
- Adhering to non-negotiables (Chapter 4, *Must Know #15*)
- Assertive love (Chapter 4, *Must Know #6*)
- Planting the emotional seeds (Chapter 4, *Must Know #19*)
- Validation (Chapter 4, *Must Know #25*)
- *Recognizing the micro-successes/gifts of recovery (see below)
- *Recovery fellowship (see below)
- *Spirituality (see below)

Recognizing the micro-successes

I refer to micro-successes as small forward steps, slight growth spurts, or little changes that can take place in the recovery process, especially in Phases 1 and 2 of treatment. Clients and family members often expect drastic changes to take place once they enter treatment, believing it to be the cure and panacea for their struggles. As you recall, I believe treatment is not designed to cure (not that it's impossible) but rather, to allow people to stabilize, move towards a healthier baseline, provide healthy options and skills, build healthy habits, and offer a preview of what a healthier lifestyle can look like. In Chapter 4, *Must Know #21*, I tell clients they are more than welcome to have the same lifestyle they engaged in prior to treatment. That will always be an option, but their healthy families are no longer going to support that old lifestyle. What treatment can offer is a sense of what a healthier life may feel and look like.

That is why it's essential that clients and family members become more attuned to recognizing not just big but also small changes (e.g., less blaming of others, less outright anger at family members, more productive phone calls, more considerate interactions, etc.), especially in the early phases of treatment. Affirming these small, incremental changes builds hope and increases self-efficacy (one's own belief that they can be successful). Author James Clear said, "That's the power of atomic habits. Tiny changes. Remarkable results." Basically, the mountain your loved ones are climbing isn't as daunting when family members validate gradual growth. This focus on positive changes reinforces that they are on the right path and what they are doing matters and is valued.

In early treatment, I tell family members, "If they stay on the phone one minute longer than they did last week, that is a micro-success," "If they are still in treatment one day more than they ever have been, appreciate the progress," "When they blame you for nine out of ten and not ten out of ten things that have gone wrong in their lives, that is a step forward." I even go as far as to tell families that if their loved one is faced with a dichotomy after treatment (e.g., drink or not drink alcohol, cut or not cut on self, call a substance-abusing friend or call a sober friend) and they have pause briefly to consider both choices, treatment already worked. That simple pause was not present prior to treatment, and the person would have chosen the unhealthier option in a flash. Treatment created that pause to think things through or "play the tape forward" to examine consequences (e.g., how will my family react, what do I stand to lose by making an unhealthy decision, how will it affect my sobriety date, etc.). Then I follow up by asking, "Is it worth it?" Almost always, the response is an exclamatory, "NO!" when people are in a healthier place and can see their situation more clearly. When I relay this message to clients, they are amazed that little differences such as a pause can have major implications on their recovery.

As time progresses in recovery, bigger changes and *Aha* moments may become more apparent. An *Aha* moment is an insight, knowledge, realization, or awareness that occurs, often when least expected. Sometimes these moments are random or catch people by surprise (e.g., realization that people love me, knowledge that I have self-worth, insight that I can get better, awareness that I have the opportunity to create a healthy life, etc.). These *Aha* moments are difficult to witness when your loved ones are unhealthy (e.g., depressed, anxious, distressed, resentful) or emotionally clouded by substances. The *Aha* moments become easier to discover when someone is recovering, as they are developing a clearer lens to view the world and becoming more mindful of what is happening around them.

To increase the chances of these *Aha* moments, I encourage clients to work on achieving at least three to five daily goals and to simply focus on being an "improved you," each day. Motivational Speaker Eric Thomas once advised an audience to wake up every day and *be a better version of who you were yesterday.* Keep it simple and don't overcomplicate the process.

Note, a good framework to use when setting goals is the SMART model—goals that are <u>S</u>pecific, <u>M</u>easurable, <u>A</u>chievable, <u>R</u>elevant, and <u>T</u>ime-Bound (Doran, 1981). For instance, a goal of "create a strong recovery program" is not a SMART goal. It is too general, not quantifiable, and is not timely. A goal that falls under the SMART model may be, "Attend one AA meeting per day, for the next seven days. The goal is specific (attend AA meeting), Measurable (one per day), Achievable (not too overwhelming), and Time-Bound (for next 7 days). SMART goals can lead to higher levels of self-efficacy, because people are able to attain small bouts of incremental successes, achievements, or wins, a little at a time.

Along the path of recovery, along with similar *Aha* moments, your loved ones may begin to have positive experiences or make more positive discoveries. This is known in the recovery community as receiving *gifts of recovery* or *gifts of sobriety*. Prior to treatment, clients and family members have, unfortunately, acclimated to emotional negativity, the half-glass-empty mindset, a dark outlook and a waiting for the "next shoe to drop" perspective, due to the chronic nature of what they have been going through. Their worldview lens has become murky, not allowing a field of vision for the good things around them, such as positivity, gratitude, and hopefulness. As they become healthier in treatment, their worldview lens—as well as their other senses—become more lucid, allowing appreciation for the positive aspects.

Perhaps your loved one will become more receptive to an estranged (but healthy) family member coming back into their lives, consider a job opportunity that wasn't available before, develop better memory capacity, have longer stamina when working out, etc. I tell clients these positive experiences may have been around them all along, but they didn't have the capacity to notice and engage before. Now, they can notice them more easily, along with new doors being opened due to their healthier well-being. The saying goes, there is no such thing as coincidences or random gifts in recovery. Experiences happen the way they're supposed to; be watchful and embrace these gifts when encountered.

One last gift your loved one may receive is the vibrant look, coherent speech, consistent honesty, and spiritual energy that exudes from someone who is in fully actualized recovery and sobriety. Time and time again, family members describe clients in a strong recovery program with accolades. "My daughter looks so much healthier." "Our son's language is incredibly clear and truthful." "My spouse has a freeing spirit about him I have not seen in a long time." I continually witness these amazing changes when clients truly embrace a healthier lifestyle. I have seen clients begin graduate school, get married, have families, attain full-time jobs, start a new business, etc. And I'm especially floored when I learn clients have entered the healthcare profession as a way of giving back and helping others the same way they have been helped to achieve a healthier life.

*Recovery fellowship

Throughout the book, I have talked about healthy fellowship and who or what it consists of (e.g., accountability, the treatment team, people who support the healthy narrative, etc.). Other words for fellowship are companionship, camaraderie, peer, family—any groups or entities a person perceives as a support system. More specifically, recovery fellowship can be the aforementioned people, but generally, they are also those people who are healthy themselves and can hold clients accountable to manage their mental health and addiction diseases. These people can be therapists, physicians, treatment teams, sobriety sponsors, sobriety groups, peer groups in recovery, healthy friends, and family members.

A recovery fellowship can provide a level of structure, routine, and accountability. Participating in a support meeting several times a week, calling people in a phone tree support system daily, or meeting with a therapist regularly can all provide a level or structure and routine to daily living. Additionally, this type of support system can serve as a safety net of accountability in case clients struggle, have a lapse—or worse, a relapse. These people can direct them back on track and provide emotional support in difficult times. Please refer to Chapter 7 under the *Accountability* heading for a refresher.

*Spirituality

Spirituality is another component often present with clients and families who achieve long-term success in recovery. Spirituality is a broad umbrella term that involves a focus on the spirit and soul. It may include religion or a belief in a power greater than oneself. This greater power can be a god, human nature, Mother Nature, the ocean, the universe, a greater process, etc. Spirituality can also involve a pursuit for deeper meaning and greater purpose in one's life.

Clients and family members express that spirituality is important because when they defer to a greater power, with the belief that as long as they are doing their due diligence and putting their best foot forward, what is meant to happen will be determined by the greater process (e.g., a god, Mother Nature, human nature, the universe, etc.). Spirituality can also provide deeper meaning and greater purpose in their lives, so they don't get caught up in trivial aspects (e.g., petty arguments with others, entertainment news, social media, making money) that are inconsequential compared to their recovery.

I tell clients one way to further enhance a search for deeper meaning and greater purpose in life is to be an impact person. An impact person is someone with the ability to help, assist, or change someone's life for the better. It is a large part of our human condition. Primatologist and conservationist Dr. Jane Goodall said, "You cannot get through a single day without having an impact on the world around you. What you do makes a difference, and you have to decide what kind of difference you want to make."

Sometimes, people think having an impact means they need to

do something on a grander scale (e.g., donate millions of dollars to a school, feed the homeless every weekend, preach to thousands of people). But being impactful doesn't have to be on a monumental level. I tell clients their recovery and sobriety alone can have significant impact.

One way clients in treatment have had a profound impact on others is by motivating a friend, cousin, family member, or romantic partner to get sober or enter treatment by the example they set. I've seen a parent agree to abstain from alcohol while their child was in treatment and end up giving up drinking, altogether. Families have stated that since their loved ones started treatment, they were able to sleep better and work on their own self-care. On a peer level, clients have expressed a gained sense of motivation from witnessing their peers get better in recovery, and this influenced them to persevere and work harder on their own treatment program. I tell clients their pursuit for purpose, meaning, and impact on others is at their fingertips, already byproducts of their recovery program. Best-selling authors Marc and Angel stated, "When you make a positive impact in someone else's life, you also make a positive impact in your own life."

Countless clients have also expressed how impactful The Serenity Prayer has been during recovery. The prayer begins, *God, grant me the serenity to accept the things I cannot change, the courage to change the things that I can, and the wisdom to know the difference.* For those clients who struggle with a higher power, I tell them to look at The Serenity Prayer as a wise-saying and leave out the word *God.* The main message of this prayer—to be at peace with things in life you have no power over, have strength to change things in life you can, and the insight to figure out which is which—is universal. There are many things in our lives we cannot control (e.g., other people's perceptions and behaviors, the environment, world events, etc.) and being at peace with those things and focusing on what can be controlled (e.g., one's own recovery program, attitude, belief system, values, people one surrounds self with, etc.) allows clients to have more acceptance, which then creates inner harmony.

The path to lifelong recovery may seem overwhelming and daunting, but the formula for success is not that complex. It's true that the Pre-treatment Zone, Phase 1, and Phase 2 are the most challenging, distressing, and unpredictable periods of the recovery process; yet these can be the most life-changing and foundational to long-term success. The plan designed for your loved one to get help may seem overwhelming, but in reality, it's ironically imbued with common sense. Concepts such as honesty, humility, and openness to direction and respecting the capabilities of the disease seem simple to grasp, but when you intermix emotions (e.g., fear, anxiety, confusion), dysfunctional family dynamics, varying levels of motivation to change within the support system, and differing strategies to implement the plan, the process can become challenging.

Developing a practical, step-by-step approach when dealing with the complexities of mental health disease was the spark ignited in me on a spring day during the initial outset of the global pandemic. Fraught with clients canceling appointments hour after hour, while sitting at my desk staring out in the distance through my office window, trying to find a way to remain motivated and impactful, I opened up a blank page and started typing this book—the "How To" execute the plan. Unbeknownst to me, that long stare into the distance would be the driving force in deciding (on a grander scale) to share with others my solutions on how to save lives and families and finally give this disease a run for its money. My vision at that moment was to reach those in the support system who feel nothing can be done and who may have lost all hope. This reinvigoration of optimistic energy that emerged in what was a sunny yet emotionally gloomy day re-kindled the fight in me to let families know they still have both the power and the potential to make an impactful difference in their loved ones' lives.

Chapter 10
Resources and Closing Remarks

Resources

Feel free to contact me if your family needs any further guidance in understanding the disease and what your roles should be, or if you need extra support creating the strategic plan.

Below, I've included my contact information, as well as a few resources for additional support or guidance.

Brian F. Licuanan, PhD

www.drbrianlicuanan.com

Depression & Bipolar Support Alliance (DBSA)

www.dbsalliance.org

MentalHealth.gov

www.mentalhealth.gov

National Alliance on Mental Illness (NAMI)

www.nami.org

The Substance Abuse and Mental Health Services Administration (SAMHSA)

www.samhsa.gov

254

Suicide Prevention Hotline

suicidepreventionlifeline.org

World Health Organization

https://www.who.int/news-room/
fact-sheets/detail/mental-disorders

Closing Remarks

I hope that by this point in the book, you are feeling empowered and knowledgeable about the things you can do as a family to get your loved ones into treatment.

Please remember, the findings presented are not theories or hypotheses, but rather, actual cases and observations from real families (like yours) who were able to get their struggling members help and direct them toward a path of long-term recovery. The information presented was drawn from my work with hundreds of clients and family units, differentiating between those who were successful in pre-treatment, the treatment process, and long-term recovery, and those who, unfortunately, weren't. Here, I share the most prominent factors and patterns that consistently emerged in my clinical work.

I strived to present the information in a clear and easy-to-follow manner, as the diseases of mental illness and substance abuse thrive on complexity. When approaching any convoluted problem, keeping the strategy straightforward and simple can be the most effective approach. My goal was to expose the disease's complexities and present an uncomplicated fight plan to take it on.

Thank you for allowing me to share my collective insights, knowledge, and recommendations. All of you have the skills, abilities, and resolve to make this journey a success. Remember, nothing comes easy during this process. It will take grit, grind, and resilience to confront this disease head on. Aim to win not only the day, but the entire war.

I am proud of you for caring enough to not give up on your loved ones. They need you more than you know, and your family can come together and be more unified than you have ever been. This disease is worried! As you educate yourselves, come together, and devise a plan, the disease grows fearful that you are creating a solidified front to take back your loved ones.

Good! That's exactly what we want!

My thoughts and wishes for courage and unrelenting strength are with you all.

Acknowledgments

This book would not have been possible without the collective support and insight from a team of people in my life ranging from family members, relatives, friends, advisors, faculty members, colleagues, book reviewers, former clients and their devoted family members. Every person contributed an important dose of knowledge, whether it be helping me in better understanding myself as a person and a clinician or allowing me the ability to embrace an even more heightened sensitivity to mental health.

First and foremost, I want to thank all my clients and their family members who humbly entrusted me to care for their most urgent needs. Their openness to my guidance meant so much to me in developing into a well-informed clinician and was the driving force to why this book was written in the first place. Second, I want to recognize and appreciate the professionals in the field who have provided me the educational and clinical foundation in shaping myself into the psychologist I am today, especially Dr. Rockey Robbins, Dr. Arnie Abels, Dr. Laura Forsyth, Dr. Lynette Sparkman-Barnes, and Dr. Richard Granese. Third, I am so grateful to all the Subject Matter Experts and reviewers (former clients and their family members) who have offered their expertise and feedback in order to ensure that the content of my book is sound and valid. Additionally, to my book editor and business consultant, Mary Vensel White. Your depth of knowledge and business acumen in the writing and publishing arenas have been invaluable to this book's success; you've been a pleasure and so fun to collaborate with. Your patience with my nitpickiness is bar none over the top. Patty Uy, your proofreading skills made my book read fluidly for my readers. And, to my graphic designer, Justin Mincks, your creativity helped accentuate certain messages I wanted to convey to the readers. Additionally, thank you, Damonza, for your diligence with formatting and amazing creativity with my book cover design. Moreover, thank you, again, Dr. Michael Mumford for affording me the opportunity to share with you the emotional quagmire I was in and helping me further realize that I was not pursuing my destined career path and that my heart was meant to help others in a clinical capacity; this decision led you in supporting my transition next door to the Counseling Department. Our conversation in the conference room that weekday afternoon feels like yesterday; please know that decision changed my life in the most positive way, and I can't express enough of my appreciation.

Additionally, to my closest inner circle of friends (VJ, Ivan, Dean, Jun, Francisco, and Juvan) whose texts and hilarious videos on our group threads provide me the laughter to get through each day. Last, I can't convey enough gratitude to my wife, Tina, and two kiddos, Chloe and Christian, and all of my family—Dad, Mom, Jay, and Tiff—who believe and champion me in my life pursuits. I know it was not always a straight path but know that your unconditional acceptance and positivity have been game changers for me, and this book would have never come to fruition without each and every one of your instrumental presences in my life.

References

American Psychiatric Association. (2013). *Diagnostic and statistical manual of mental health disorders*. (5th ed.). Washington, DC.

American Psychological Association (2023). *Disease*. APA Dictionary of Psychology. *https://dictionary.apa.org/disease*

Aristotle (2019). *Aristotle's Nicomachean Ethics* (3rd ed). Hackett Publishing Company, Inc. benlionelscott1.[@benlionelscott1]. (2022). *Push through it. Spoken by Eric Thomas.* [Video]. TikTok. *https://www.tiktok.com/@benlionelscott1/* video/7076705858159136001

Berman, P. & Goodall, J. (1999). *Reason for hope: A spiritual journey*. Grand Central Publishing.

BetterHelp. (2023). *Willpower: Definition and how to increase it. https://www.betterhelp.com/advice/willpower/ willpower-definition-and-how-to-increase-it/*

Celebrate Recovery. (2023). *Prayer for Serenity. https://www.celebraterecovery.com/resources/serenity-prayer*

Chernoff, A. & Chernoff, M. (2019). *1000+ Little things happy successful people do differently*. TarcherPerigree.

Clear, J. (2015) *Atomic habits: An easy & proven way to build good habits & break bad ones.*

Random House Business Books.

Collins Dictionary. (n.d.). Desperation. In *Collinsdictionary.com dictionary*.
Retrieved November 27, 2023, from https://www. collinsdictionary.com/*dictionary/english/desperation/related*

Comtois, K.A. (2002). A review of interventions to reduce the prevalence of parasuicide.
Psychiatric Services, 53 (9), 1138-1144.

Doran, G.T. (1981). Theres a SMART way to write management's goals and objectives. *Journal of Management Review,* 70, 35-36.

Dictionary. (n.d.). Risk Factor. In *Dictionary.com dictionary*. Retrieved November 27, 2023, from *https://www.dictionary.com/ browse/risk-factor*

Dunne, C. (2015). *Carl Jung: Wounded healer of the soul.* Watkins Publishing. etthehiphoppreacher (2015, September 8), *Eric Thomas; You owe you* [Video].
You Tube. *https://www.youtube.com/watch?v=7Oxz060iedY*

The Haynes Clinic. (2023). *I Am Your Disease. https://thehaynesclinic. com/addictions-in-general/i-am-your-disease/*

Merriam-Webster Dictionary. (n.d.). Culture. In *Merriam-webster. com dictionary*.
Retrieved November 27, 2023, from *https://www. merriamwebster.com/dictionary/culture*

Merriam-Webster Dictionary. (n.d.). Disease. In *Merriam-webster. com dictionary*.
Retrieved November 27, 2023, from https://www.merriam-*webster.com/dictionary/ disease#:~:text=noun,signs%20and%20 symptoms%20%3A%20sickness%2C%20malady*

Merriam-Webster Dictionary. (n.d.). Guilt. In *Merriam-webster.com dictionary*.

Retrieved November 27, 2023, from *https://www.merriam-webster.com/dictionary/guilt* Merriam-Webster Dictionary. (n.d.). In *Merriam-webster.com dictionary.*
Retrieved November 27, 2023, from Humility. https://www. merriam-*webster.com/ dictionary/humility*

National Harm Reduction Coalition. (2023). *Harm reduction. https://recoveryohio.gov/priorities/initial- report-1/5-harm-reduction*

Oxford English Dictionary. (n.d.). Amends. In *oed.com dictionary.* Retrieved November 27, 2023, from *https://www.oed.com/search/ dictionary/?scope= Entries&q=amends*

Oxford English Dictionary. (n.d.). Stigma. In *oed.com dictionary.*

Retrieved November 27, 2023, from *https://www.oed.com/search/ dictionary/?scope= Entries&q=stigma*

Oxford English Dictionary. (n.d.). Trust. In *oed.com dictionary.* Retrieved November 27, 2023, from *https://www.oed.com/search/dict ionary/?scope=Entries&q=trust&tl=true*

Prochaska, J.O. & DiClemente, C.C. (1982) Transtheoretical therapy: Toward a more integrative model of change. *Psychotherapy: Theory, Research and Practice*, 19: 276-288.

Pursuit of Purpose. (2022, November 9), *When you do things in life that are easy, life will be hard....* [Video]. You Tube. *https://www. youtube.com/shorts/xj0aQnnVJUU*

Robbins, Tony (2022), *Progress equals happiness* [Video]. You Tube, *https://www.youtube.com/watch?v=Z_nalShHuJY*

Shannon, Joseph (2016, April 28). *Reasoning with unreasonable people: Focus on disorders of emotional regulation* [Conference presentation]. Continuing Education Seminar, Irvine, CA, United States.

Spooners Motivation. (2022, December 7), *If you could look up, you could get up* [Video]. You Tube. *https://www.youtube.com/shorts/jX-5ZsIiEqo*

Substance Abuse and Mental Health Services Administration (2020). *SAMHSA's working definition of recovery. SAMHSA. https://store.samhsa.gov/sites/default/files/pep12-recdef.pdf*

Substance Abuse and Mental Health Services Administration (2020). *Risk and protective factors.*

SAMHSA. *https://www.samhsa.gov/sites/default/files/20190718-samhsa-risk-protective-factors.pdf*
Vidbi (2016), *Denzel Washington—University of Pennsylvania* [Video]. You Tube.
https://www.youtube.com/watch?v=JEFbfwg9dek

Words for You (2022), *Inspirational Vince Lombardi quotes that will motivate you* [Video]. You Tube. *https://www.youtube.com/watch?v=BOr021fpha8*

9 7 9 8 9 8 7 8 3 0 9 8 7